OLD SHITE'S
ALMANAC

OLD SHITE'S
ALMANAC

A. PARODY

MICHAEL O'MARA BOOKS LIMITED

First published in Great Britain in 2006 by
Michael O'Mara Books Limited
9 Lion Yard
Tremadoc Road
London SW4 7NQ

This paperback edition first published in 2007

A CIP catalogue record for this book is available from the British Library

Papers used by Michael O'Mara Books Limited are natural, recyclable
products made from wood grown in sustainable forests. The manufacturing
processes conform to the environmental regulations of the country of origin.

ISBN: 978-1-84317-276-5

10 9 8 7 6 5 4 3 2 1

www.mombooks.com

Designed and typeset by Design 23

Printed and bound in Great Britain by Cox and Wyman, Reading, Berks

SOME INTERESTING CONTENTS
(WITH THEIR PAGE NUMBERS)

FROM PRE-PUBLICATION REVIEWS OF
OLD SHITE'S ALMANAC

'Although Parody's discursion upon coefficients of linear expansion in alloys such as phosphor-bronze is never less than first-rate, it is in the inclusion of contemporary eyewitness material relating to enforced homosexuality (admittedly, in carceral situations) inflicted upon the latter-day Cathars that this text truly shines.'
SANDY ARBUTHNOT, *Seattle Times Literary Supplement*

'Another winner from Mr Parody. *Old Shite's Almanac,* with its comprehensive review of some of the events of part of 2006, is the perfect companion for a day's fishing.'
HORATIO SHUDDERINGFLUFF, *The Sturgeon*

'Ici on peut paraphraser Destouches, dans sa pièce *Le Glorieux* de 1732:
LISETTE: Mais on dit qu'aux auteurs le critique est utile . . .
PHILINTE: La critique est aisée, et l'art est difficile.
Au fond, je devine que M. Parody est un anthologue épouvantable.'
H. H. CRIPPEN, MD, *Cosmopolitan* (COLOMBEY-LES-DEUX-ÉGLISES)

'An invaluable guide for the year to come, with incisive astrological analysis. I cannot envisage a time when I won't have a copy to hand.' MYSTIC REG, *Psychic Men Only*

'I cannot recommend this book enough. In fact I cannot recommend it at all.' GERALDINE UPMARKET, *What's On In Mablethorpe*

'Reading this slim volume is not unlike eating mushrooms in cold béchamel while listening to a poor recording of Stockhausen's *Helicopter Quartet* – that by the Royal Amsterdam Concertgebouw under McKerras in 1997 springs immediately to mind – it really is that good.' JOHN 'JOHNNY' JOHNSON, *The Economist*
(ALICE SPRINGS, NT, AUSTRALIA)

'F*****g great – makes *Harry Potter* look like a book for kids.'
PEREGRINE SCUMBAG, *Lists and Listmen*

'If you want to know what's going on in the world, you can either bug people's phones or buy *Old Shite's Almanac*.'

ROGER SWILL, **Daily Scrote**

'Plangent, evanescent, coruscating, sub-critical – as engrossing as the season's first Whitstables on the half-shell.'

THE HON. MRS BALLS-MCEWAN, **Big Bike** MAGAZINE

'The emotional and intellectual landscape of the Great War has never been more brilliantly evoked, while the ironical, post-Modernist deployment of consecutive "numbers" at the foot of each page made even this reviewer weep at the inevitability of it all. Forget Lionel Shriver, forget Brett Easton Ellis, forget – if you must – Dan Brown, but under no circumstances should you be without this book.'   MAJOR-GENERAL SIR EDWARD BLOUNT-FISHCAKE, KCE,

Small-to-Medium Caterer

'The book that dare not speak its name . . . '

PROFESSOR ÉDOUARD POUVANTABLE, **Moose Jaw Literary Review**

'I shudder to think . . . '   LORD PEEBLES,* **Tarmac Review**

'A masterpiece of literature. Brilliantly researched, erudite, concise and informative.'   ALBERT SNOUT, **Practical Pigbreeder**

'Read it from cover to cover then fry it in breadcrumbs.'

CAPTAIN BIRDSEYE, **Savoury Delights Bulletin**

'Miles better than the stuff we come out with.'

IVAN OFFELCOFF, **Phlegm Fortnightly**

*Reginald Otterburn St Agnes Carroll, thirteenth Viscount Peebles, *b.* 1921

Entry from *Who's Who 2009: 161st annual edition* (suppressed on the instructions of the Lord Chancellor, the Attorney-General, the Solicitor-General, the Treasury Solicitor, the Department of Public Prosecutions, the Chief Constable, Strathclyde Police, and the Procurator-Fiscal, Glasgow)

PARODY, Professzor-Doktor Antal; polymath, writer, artist, musician, scientist, inventor, engineer, oenophile, marksman, equestrian, aviator, hero, genius and patriot; instigator of the 'Mashed-Potato Revolution', Budapest, 1947; Visiting Professor in Applied Rubber Engineering, Catholic University of Cape Wrath, since 1972; Honorary Professor of Aviation Musicology, University of Little Fork (VA), 1998; *b* (as Count Antal Vajk Árpád György Tamás Pál István Parodí) 23 April 1921, Székesfehérvár, Fejer, Hungary, *oc* of Colonel-General Count Villö Parodí, and Lady Fiona Parodí, MC (*née* Kray-Smith, *ed* of late 4th Earl of Andersonstown, *qv.*); *m* 1st 1942 Emilie, Gräfin von und zu Düsseldorf und Untergürgl (marriage diss. 1942), widow of late Rittmeister Albrecht, Graf von und zu Düsseldorf und Untergürgl; 2nd 1948 William Bastard (marriage annulled on grounds of mistaken identity 1948), *oc* of Mr and the late Mrs Eric Bastard, 1 *s*, 2 *d* (all adoptive); 3rd 2003 Mrs Sheila ('Dag') Emu, *yd* of Mr Nobby Emu of Barbie Rocks, NSW. Educ. Gyór Military Acad.; St István's Seminary for the Sons of Distressed Officers (declined to take Holy Orders); Royal Hungarian University (MSc 1940, PhD 1942). Served War of 1939–45 in various theatres (principally revues in Paris and, later, London); Order of St Elizabeth the Impossibly Tiny with Daggers, 1946. Numerous substantive and honorary posts in higher-educational establishments throughout Free Europe; Chairman, Anglo-Magyar Labrador Retriever Club of Great Britain and Northern Ireland (But Not Wales), 1968–73 (Dickin Medal, 1969); retired to devote more time to writing and to scientific and philosophical activities; stood unsuccessfully as 'Action for Blindly Unthinking Patriotism' candidate in elections to European Parliament, 1999; Governor, Droppings Acad., since 1951. *Publications:* Shite's Unoriginal Miscellany, 2003; Eats, Shites & Leaves: Crap English and How To Use It, 2004; Shitedoku, 2005; A Shite History of Nearly Everything, 2005; They Think It's All Shite . . . It Is Now!: An Alternative Guide to the World Cup; numerous articles in scientific, philosophical, philological, psychiatric, entomological, etc. journals, letters to newspapers, telegrams to world leaders, e-mails to supermodels etc. *Recreations:* patriotism, mashed potato, seal culling, hurling abuse, being a genius. *Address:* c/o Michael O'Mara Books Limited. *Clubs:* Imperial Austro-Hungarian (Vienna); Sebastian's Little Hole (Cannes); Kennel Club of Great Britain (Hon. Overseas Member); Rhodesian Blazers (Harare [formerly Salisbury], Zimbabwe [formerly Southern Rhodesia]).

See also Earl of Andersonstown, Hon. Reginald Kray-Smith, Graf von und zu Düsseldorf und Untergürgl

WHAT THEY SAY ABOUT *OLD SHITE'S ALMANAC*

Mrs Myrtle Frogspawn of Chipping Sodbury says:

'I just can't put *Old Shite's Almanac* down – at least not since I got superglue on my fingers.'

•

Mrs Joan Grundy of East Kilbride says:

'My life has changed since I started reading *Old Shite's Almanac* – previously I was Mr John Grundy.'

•

Mr Sidney Moose of Pontefract says:

'When I followed the football pools tips in a rival almanac, I lost £900 in a year. But with *Old Shite's Almanac*, I lost only £875.'

•

Mrs Ruby Sidesalad of Hemel Hempstead says:

'I always keep a copy of *Old Shite's Almanac* in the bathroom – the paper's so much softer than Izal.'

•

Mrs Tina Hornet of Aberdare says:

'Before I read your book, my husband and I had been trying for a baby for years. But thanks to Old Shite's words of wisdom, since 1988 I have been pregnant by every man in our street.'

INTRODUCTION

When William Caxton introduced the printing press to England in 1476, one of the first things he did was to ask his good friend Emmanuel Parody what sort of book should test his new machine. Displaying wisdom beyond his eighty-nine years, Parody suggested an almanac chronicling events of the year just gone, making astrological predictions for the year ahead and recording some things that might have happened if other things hadn't happened first. Thus was born *Old Shite's Almanac*, now in its 531st year and still as irrelevant as ever. Down the centuries, generations of Parodys demonstrated admirable prescience to prophesy such world-changing events as the Fall of the Berlin Wall and the Great Fire of London, although rival almanacs have churlishly pointed out that Seamus Parody helped build the former and that Sebastian Parody served ten years for the latter. As I am Emmanuel's only living descendant, the burden of safeguarding the planet on an annual basis has now fallen on my frail shoulders, but when I gazed into my crystal balls twelve months ago, how could I have known how accurate my premonitions would prove? For I correctly foretold that in 2006 there would be a World Cup, that John Prescott would be revealed as having an affair with a woman with the initials TT (admittedly I thought it would be Tina Turner) and that I wouldn't be invited to my next-door neighbour's birthday party. So to discover what lies ahead in your life, as predicted by the stars and a lonely man in a one-roomed flat, there really is no substitute for *Old Shite's Almanac*.

ANTAL PARODY

THE DANGEROUS BOOK FOR MUMMY'S BOYS

Pursuits include:
Hoop-la   Doing your homework   Skipping
Helping with the dishes   Hopscotch   Tidying your room
Scrabble (no rude words)   Filing your nails   Embroidery

THINGS YOU LEARN WHEN YOU HAVE CHILDREN

Teddy bears can climb in and block the toilet all by themselves.

Eventually, you *can* find a biscuit, cookie or cracker that the DVD player will accept.

Small pieces of Lego will ultimately pass through a toddler's digestive system.

There *is* room to swing a cat in your lounge.

Stray Mutant Ninja Turtle weaponry is attracted to bare feet.

Extractor fans can be used to chop bananas.

The police arrive before the fire brigade.

The nearest A&E is too far to drive with a broken arm.

In any stone-throwing contest, the windows lose.

A ceiling fan will not spin a four-year-old Batman dangling from a dog's lead.

Fights do not end just because you say so.

Kitty litter turns into a swamp monster when poured down the loo.

A pillow case is rubbish as a parachute.

Kids' shoes are just as comfortable on the wrong feet.

PROVERBS

Never bolt your door with a boiled carrot.
IRISH PROVERB

It's when it's small that the cucumber gets warped.
PORTUGUESE PROVERB

Nobody lifts the dog's tail when it defecates.
THAI PROVERB

All the goats jump onto leaning trees.
POLISH PROVERB

The only free cheese is in the mousetrap.
RUSSIAN PROVERB

Two watermelons can't be grabbed in one hand.
AFGHAN PROVERB

A dried fish cannot be used as a cat's pillow.
CHINESE PROVERB

A one-eyed uncle is better than no uncle at all.
BENGALI PROVERB

It's the merry drizzle that makes grass grow fine.
ITALIAN PROVERB

The donkey only dances if its well-being is exceptional.
HUNGARIAN PROVERB

The badger is not aware of its own blaze.
SIBERIAN PROVERB

Claw a churl by the breech, and he will shite in your fist.
FRENCH PROVERB

It is better not to poke a jaguar with a short staff.
BRAZILIAN PROVERB

Wormy beans will have blind buyers.
TURKISH PROVERB

Bare walls make giddy housekeepers.
IRISH PROVERB

The shrimp that sleeps gets carried by the tide.
MEXICAN PROVERB

You can't straighten a dog's tail by putting it in a hosepipe.
INDIAN PROVERB

Who reaches for the spruce falls down onto the juniper.
FINNISH PROVERB

The crow does not take the eye out of another crow.
GREEK PROVERB

A bird that flies from the ground onto an anthill does not know
that it is still on the ground.
NIGERIAN PROVERB

The wolf has a thick neck because he does his job on his own.
BULGARIAN PROVERB

Fine words butter no parsnips.
ENGLISH PROVERB

It is better to shoot your wife and child than to spill
a drop of alcohol.
GERMAN PROVERB

Add legs to the snake after you have finished drawing it.
CHINESE PROVERB

Who wants yoghurt in winter must carry a cow in his pocket.
TURKISH PROVERB

The will of the heart is to hug the mountain, but the arm
is not long enough.
INDONESIAN PROVERB

There is hope as long as your fishing line is in the water.
NORWEGIAN PROVERB

A dog that has been bitten by a snake fears the sausage.
PORTUGUESE PROVERB

The lizard that swallows doesn't vomit.
SPANISH PROVERB

Bring a cow into the hall and she'll run the byre.
SCOTTISH PROVERB

Don't sell the skin of the bear from the forest.
ROMANIAN PROVERB

In the shallowest waters, the ugliest fish swim.
SWEDISH PROVERB

It is usually dark below the candlestick.
CZECH PROVERB

He who bends over too far shows his rear end.
CORSICAN PROVERB

Every sandpiper praises his own swamp.
RUSSIAN PROVERB

A coat twice turned is not worth sleeving.
IRISH PROVERB

Carefulness is the mother of the porcelain cabinet.
DUTCH PROVERB

SOME STORIES FROM 2006
THAT YOU MAY HAVE MISSED

Having experienced problems maintaining an erection, a Serbian man hit upon the bright idea of inserting a thin pencil into his penis to keep it stiff during sex. Unfortunately for Zeljko Tupic, the evening was a write-off because the pencil slipped and became lodged in his bladder, forcing him to undergo emergency surgery at a Belgrade hospital.

•

A burly Croatian lumberjack announced his intention to sue his local health authority after a kidney transplant left him addicted to housework and knitting. Stjepan Lizacic said he had not been warned about the possible side effects of being given the kidney of a fifty-year-old woman. He complained: 'I used to enjoy heavy drinking sessions with my pals, but now I have developed a strange passion for female jobs like ironing, sewing, washing dishes, sorting clothes in wardrobes and even knitting. My wife is the only one that is pleased.'

•

A fire broke out during an operation at a New Zealand hospital after the patient broke wind at an inopportune moment. The man, who was at the Southern Cross Hospital in Invercargill to have haemorrhoids removed, suffered minor burns in the incident. The fire was caused by methane in his flatulence igniting a spark from the electrical machine that was being used to remove his piles.

•

To demonstrate his love for his girlfriend, Hannes Pisek made a huge heart out of 220 burning candles on the floor of his flat in Hoenigsberg, Austria. Unfortunately, while he was collecting her from work his burning heart set fire to the flat. He lost not only his home but also his girl, who dumped him and moved back in with her parents.

•

A mongrel dog with a talent for fetching lost balls was awarded lifetime membership of his local golf club. Deuce was rewarded for returning over 3,000 balls to members of Pontnewydd Golf Club in South Wales. But he is still the only member not allowed in the clubhouse, because dogs are banned.

An Indian man with a 13-inch tail has become an object of worship, but still can't find a wife. Chandre Oram from West Bengal is regarded by locals as an incarnation of Hindu monkey god Hanuman, but the tail, which he has refused to have surgically removed, proves something of a turn-off for the ladies. He laments: 'Almost twenty women have turned down marriage proposals. They see me and agree, but as soon as I turn around, they see my tail and leave.'

•

An American pensioner tried to smoke out a nest of raccoons in his attic, but ended up burning down his house instead.
C. W. Roseburr from Kansas City went into the attic armed with a kerosene-soaked rag on a stick, but his actions led to the eaves catching fire. Afterwards, a defiant Mr Roseburr insisted: 'I set the raccoon on fire. He's the one that set the house on fire.'

•

A cyclist who had travelled 335,500 miles on the same bike had it stolen as soon as he arrived in Britain. German Heinz Stucke has journeyed to 165 countries since buying the bike in 1962, but it was stolen just hours after he landed in Portsmouth en route for Greenland. Happily, it was found abandoned in a local park the next day.

•

Sixteen-year-old Carly O'Brien wanted her wedding day to be bigger than Jordan's, but the teenage Gloucester bride chose such a vast wedding dress that she got stuck in the church door for an hour and a half. Carly's £25,000 dress was 8 feet wide, had a 60-foot-long train and weighed 25 stone. The combined efforts of twenty people eventually managed to push her through the door and up the aisle, and another fourteen (plus the groom) had to carry her out again at the end of the ceremony.

•

A Turkish shop assistant was arrested after being found lying naked with a mannequin in a shop window. Staff who arrived to open the store in Antalya called police after spotting bite marks on the dummy. Two other mannequins that showed signs of abuse were also seized as evidence.

Soccer fan Paul Hucker paid £100 to insure himself for £1 million against the trauma of seeing England knocked out in the early stages of the World Cup.

•

A mild-mannered Miami accountant was revealed to be a descendant of the infamous thirteenth-century Mongolian warlord Genghis Khan. Genetic testing showed that forty-eight-year-old Tom Robinson was related to the man who rampaged across Asia, killing thousands in his wake. Mr Robinson commented: 'Obviously I've done nothing as big as Genghis Khan. I haven't conquered any countries, although I have headed up accounting groups.'

•

Chip-makers at the McCain factory in Scarborough were forced to evacuate the premises after discovering that one of their potatoes was actually a hand grenade. The grenade, spotted among a pile of potatoes that were being cleaned, was destroyed in a controlled explosion. The potatoes came from fields in northern France and Belgium, prompting a McCain spokesman to comment: 'It is something that we will be looking into with our suppliers.'

•

A Leeds man discovered that his girlfriend was cheating on him after his pet parrot repeatedly said another man's name. Chris Taylor became suspicious because Ziggy the parrot squawked, 'Hiya, Gary' in a female voice whenever Suzy Collins's mobile rang. The bird also made kissing noises on hearing the name Gary on TV. When confronted, Suzy admitted she had been seeing Gary for four months. Following the break-up of the relationship, Ms Collins confessed: 'I couldn't stand Ziggy and it looks now like the feeling was mutual.'

•

Yahaya Wahib received a phone bill for £125 trillion from Telekom Malaysia for recent calls on his dead father's line. After initially giving him ten days to pay up or face prosecution, the company was said to be looking into the matter.

•

Marian Morris, a retired nurse from Arkansas, rescued her brother's pet chicken by giving it the kiss of life. Seeing Boo Boo floating face down in a pond, she sprang into action. 'I breathed into its beak and its eyes popped open,' she recalled.

A Greek student living in England turned her grandmother into a living sculpture at a Leeds art exhibition. Janis Rafailidous put her eighty-year-old granny, Athena, into a mock-up kitchen where visitors could watch her cleaning, chopping food and knitting.

•

Newspaper reports revealed that an Indian man had spent the past fifty years living in a tree following a row with his wife. Gayadhar Parida took refuge in a mango tree following a trivial quarrel with his wife back in 1956. But he enjoyed the peace and solitude so much that even after his tree house was destroyed by a storm, he elected to move to another tree rather than go back home.

•

A Sudanese man was ordered to marry a goat after being caught having sex with the animal. When the goat's owner, a Mr Alifi, witnessed the unsavoury liaison, he arranged for the man to pay him a £40 dowry for the goat 'because he used it as his wife'. Mr Alifi helpfully told reporters: 'I have given him the goat, and as far as I know they are still together.'

•

Jesse Maggrah decided to go for a stroll on Canadian Pacific Railway tracks near Red Deer, Alberta while listening to heavy metal music through earphones. Perhaps not surprisingly, he was soon hit from behind by a train. Luckily, he suffered nothing worse than broken ribs and was able to reflect: 'Maybe the metal gods above were smiling on me, and they didn't want one of their true warriors to die on them.'

•

An Austrian dog owner revealed that his pet dachshund has been getting through ten cigarettes a day for the past seventeen years. Wolfgang Treitler said the twenty-two-year-old dog, General Edi, is addicted to nicotine. 'He eats the tobacco and the paper, and then chews a while on the filter before spitting it out. But all of his teeth are fine, and he is as fit as a puppy.'

•

A Yorkshireman survived a 30-foot fall from a mill chimney because he had the good fortune to land in a pile of pigeon poo. Phil Harrison was trying to rescue a friend's hawk when he went crashing down to the basement, but, although he broke his neck, the impact was cushioned by the 6-inch layer of bird droppings.

Romanian football team Regal Hornia demanded compensation after a defender they had signed for 15 kg of pork sausages walked out on the club the following day. The Fourth Division outfit used up its week's sausage allowance to sign defender Marius Cioara from UT Arad but the sausage taunts proved too much for him and he announced that he was going to work on a farm in Spain.

•

A Swedish orchestra that plays instruments carved from blocks of ice had to abandon a performance in an igloo when one of the flutes started to melt. The curtailment was blamed on the flautist's hot breath.

•

A mugger who stole a World Cup ticket from a woman's handbag was arrested after sitting down to watch the game next to the victim's husband. The thief robbed Eva Standmann as she was on her way to the Munich stadium to watch Australia play Brazil. Discovering the ticket in her handbag, the mugger decided to use her seat, but as he sat down, her husband Berndt alerted security.

•

A pet fish was blamed for starting a fire which destroyed a house in Poole, Dorset. Kipper, a 20 cm catfish, sparked the blaze during a fight with another fish in his tank. Water splashed out of the aquarium onto an electric plug, sending a power surge up the tank's light cable. This burned the plastic lid, which then melted and dripped onto a leather sofa, setting it alight. The family survived, but the fish perished in the inferno.

•

A Ryanair flight from Liverpool to Derry landed instead at a military base five miles away after the pilot mistook it for the international airport. Passengers described how excited soldiers rushed out to greet the plane as it touched down at the Ballykelly base. 'They couldn't believe what was happening,' said one, 'and neither could we!'

•

With echoes of the fairy tale, a Canadian woman arrived home to find a bear eating porridge in her kitchen. The bear devoured oatmeal from a container that it had opened before wandering back into the West Vancouver woods.

A pair of Serbian petrol station attendants on night shift slept while thieves broke into their office and escaped with a safe weighing 50 stone. The gang ripped the safe from the wall and dragged it out of the building, making enough noise to wake the dead, but not these two. It was only when the morning shift arrived that the robbery was discovered.

•

Australian artist Tim Patch paints portraits of politicians using his penis as a brush – probably the first case of a member being painted by one. After first revealing his talent at a New Year's Eve party, Patch has gone on to make several exhibitions of himself. Wisely perhaps, Rolf Harris elected for more traditional methods when painting his portrait of the Queen.

•

An elderly Polish man was chained up by his wife in a dog kennel for three weeks because she was fed up with him arriving home drunk. After his vodka habit incurred the wrath of wife Helena, seventy-five-year-old Zdislawa Bukarowicza had to survive in freezing temperatures wrapped in an old blanket and existing on a diet of dog food and water. He was freed only after his drinking friends, worried by his absence, notified the police.

•

A Chinese man attracted bids from fifty-eight would-be buyers when he attempted to sell his soul online. Taobao, China's leading Internet auction site, eventually stopped the sale because it wanted proof that the seller could actually provide the goods. A spokesman said: 'He must provide written permission from a higher authority.'

•

Unable to settle a debt of £1,800, a Romanian man handed over his wife as repayment instead. Emil Iancu signed a document saying that wife Daniela would live with elderly creditor Jozef Justien Lostrie and, far from being aggrieved, Mrs Iancu was full of praise for the arrangement. She said: 'Before I had to clean the house and look after our three children on my own, while Emil did nothing, but now I'm treated like a guest and hardly have to raise a finger.'

•

Two English football fans in Cologne for the World Cup took the precaution of writing down the street name *Einbahn Strasse* so that they could remember where they'd parked their car. But on returning, they found that every second street in the inner city was called *Einbahn Strasse*, which, unknown to them, means 'one-way street'. They eventually located their car several hours later with help from German police.

•

When social workers in Germany received a call from an anxious mother urging them to curb her wayward daughter's loose morals, they were in for a shock. For the daughter turned out to be sixty-eight! Adelheid Schmidt, ninety-two, contacted social services after learning that daughter Tina had a boyfriend, but they said there was nothing they could do as her 'child' was fifty years too old for their involvement.

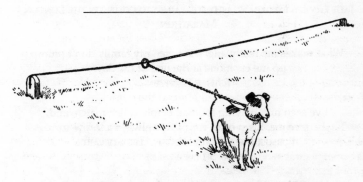

A method of allowing a dog to take exercise without being at liberty.
Two short posts are driven into the ground, a considerable distance
apart and a stout wire is strained over them for the ring, to which the
dog's chain is attached.
NB: not suitable for training greyhounds.

THE DA VINCI CODE: A SUMMARY OF THE TRIAL

'You copied my book.'
'Didn't.'
'Did.'
'Didn't.'

QUOTES OF THE YEAR

'I couldn't be more chuffed if I were a badger at the start of
the mating season.'
QUEENS PARK RANGERS MANAGER IAN HOLLOWAY
AFTER HIS TEAM BEAT CARDIFF CITY

'It doesn't matter how gym-toned the girl might be, there is
still something about her that looks like she was designed to
bring in the washing.'
JENNY ECLAIR, ON COLEEN MCLOUGHLIN

'I don't really understand miles – I didn't actually know how
far it was going to be.'
JADE GOODY, EXPLAINING WHY SHE FAILED TO COMPLETE THE LONDON
MARATHON

'What makes me really angry is when my family don't plump
up the cushions at the end of the day.'
ESTHER RANTZEN

'I've seen him playing football before a Test match, and,
believe me, his second touch was always a throw-in.'
FORMER ENGLAND CRICKETER ALEC STEWART
ON SHANE WARNE

'An OBE is what you get if you clean the toilets well at
King's Cross station.'
MICHAEL WINNER, DECLINING THE HONOUR

'We've got three fridges – food in one, salad in another and drinks
in the third. In the drinks one, everything is symmetrical. If there
are three cans of Diet Coke, he'd throw one away rather than
having three, because it has to be an even number.'
VICTORIA BECKHAM ON HUSBAND DAVID'S OBSESSION WITH NEATNESS

'I am not married to David Beckham. I am not even engaged to him.'
SVEN-GÖRAN ERIKSSON, SCOTCHING THE RUMOURS ONCE AND FOR ALL

GONE BUT NOT FORGOTTEN, 2006

Tony Banks
Peter Benchley
Robert Carrier
Desmond Dekker
Eddie, the dog from *Frasier*
J.K. Galbraith
Freddie Garrity (of Freddie and the Dreamers)
Ron Greenwood
Harriet, a 175-year-old Giant Galapagos tortoise
Charles Haughey
Jimmy Johnstone
John Junkin
Brian Labone
Sir Freddie Laker
Al Lewis (Grandpa in *The Munsters*)
John Lyall
Henry McGee
Slobodan Milosevic
Peter Osgood
Jackie Pallo
Floyd Patterson
Lynne Perrie
Wilson Pickett
Gene Pitney
Billy Preston
John Profumo
Lou Rawls
Linda Smith
Dame Muriel Spark
Aaron Spelling
Fred Trueman
Dennis Weaver
Caspar Weinberger
Jack Wild
Shelley Winters

FORGOTTEN BUT NOT GONE

Gary Barlow
'Nasty Nick' Bateman
Emma Bunton
David Dickinson
Iain Duncan Smith
Gareth Gates
Julie Goodyear
Charles Kennedy
John Kerry
Anthea Turner
Pete Waterman

HUTTON REVISITED

The decision by the judge in the trial concerning *The Da Vinci Code* to incorporate a code of his own into the official ruling was apparently not an isolated incident. It prompted us to take a closer look at the conclusion to the Hutton Report.

(4)(A)(i) There was no dishonourable or underhand or duplicitous strategy by the Government covertly to leak Dr Kelly's name to the media. If the bare details of the MoD statement dated 8 July 2003, the changing drafts of the Q and A material prepared in the MoD, and the lobby briefings by the Prime Minister's spokesman on 9 July are looked at in isolation from the surrounding circumstances it would be possible to infer, as some commentators have done, that there was an underhand strategy by the Government to leak Dr Kelly's name in a covert way. However, having heard a large volume of evidence on this issue I have concluded that there was no such strategy on the part of the Government. I consider that in the midst of a major controversy relating to Mr Gilligan's broadcasts which had contained very grave allegations against the integrity of the Government and fearing that Dr Kelly's name as the source for those broadcasts would be disclosed by the media at any time, the Government's main concern was that it would be charged with a serious cover up if it did not reveal that a civil servant had come forward. I consider that the evidence of Mr Donald Anderson MP and Mr Andrew Mackinlay MP, the Chairman and a member respectively of the FAC, together with the questions put by Sir John Stanley MP to Dr Kelly when he appeared before the FAC, clearly show that the Government's concern was well founded.'

LEAST POPULAR FUNERAL SONGS FOR 2006

'Congratulations'
'Going Underground'
'Staying Alive'
'Oh Happy Day'
'Hole in the Ground'
'Body Talk'

SOME PEOPLE WHO WERE OVERLOOKED FOR THE JOB OF ENGLAND FOOTBALL MANAGER IN 2006

Christopher Biggins
Basil Brush
Albert Einstein
Michael Buerk
Esther Rantzen
The Chuckle Brothers
Harry Hill
Thomas Cranmer

THE METATARSAL – A CONCISE HISTORY

Until 2002 most people in England thought the metatarsal came between the Mesozoic and the Jurassic. But when David Beckham broke his second metatarsal that April and was in such pain that he could barely make it to the hairdresser's, we learned that it was one of five bones leading to the toes.

Beckham was just about fit enough for the 2002 World Cup, but team-mate Gary Neville, who broke his fifth metatarsal around the same time, missed out. Since then, England players have repeatedly suffered from the so-called 'curse of the metatarsal'.

In May 2002 Danny Murphy fractured his fourth metatarsal; during Euro 2004 Wayne Rooney broke his fifth metatarsal; in September 2004 Steven Gerrard broke his fifth metatarsal; three months later Scott Parker fractured his second metatarsal; in October 2005 Ashley Cole broke his fifth metatarsal; in December 2005 Michael Owen broke his fifth metatarsal; in April 2006 Ledley King damaged his fourth metatarsal; and, that same month, Rooney broke the fourth metatarsal of his right foot, putting his participation in the World Cup in serious jeopardy.

Everyone from the FA to the Biggleswade & District Women's Institute held prayer vigils for his swift recovery.

As metatarsal fever mounted, BBC News 24 sought expert answers. Here is a transcript of the interview with their studio guest:

Q: I understand that the five metatarsal bones in the foot act as a unit to help share the load of the body?

A: Er, yes.

Q: And that they move position to cope with uneven ground?

A: I believe that's right.

Q: And in sport, it's the first, second and fifth metatarsals that are most commonly injured?

A: Um, yes.

Q: And that the fifth is the worst one to damage?

A: But Rooney's damaged the fourth.

Q: Yes, I appreciate that. So, in your expert opinion, what are the chances of him being fit for the World Cup?

A: Don't ask me, I'm only here to clean the office.

2006 IN BITE-SIZE . . . BUT WITH NO ANCHOVIES

CRIME
In Britain's largest cash raid, £53 million was stolen from a
Securitas depot in Kent. Some of the money was recovered after a
gang member walked into a branch of Ladbroke's and tried to bet
£30 million on the 2.30 at Towcester.

In a bid to cut instances of domestic violence, the government
introduced a 'wife amnesty', whereby husbands were given three
weeks to hand in unwanted spouses to their local police station.
Delighted Home Office officials announced that their haul
included sixty-three school headmistresses, thirty-nine doctors'
receptionists and two Conservative MPs.

POLITICS
In the biggest scandal to hit the government since David Blunkett
discovered that his grace and favour guide dog was on wheels, a
woman came forward to reveal that she had been having sex with
John Prescott through choice. Shy, private, tearful, Tracey Temple
told her story in a six-page spread in *The Mail on Sunday*,
recounting their sexual liaisons in graphic detail to a public trying
to hold down its Sunday lunch. The unsavoury episode earned
Prescott a new nickname of 'Two Shags'.

The Liberal Democrats received a massive boost to the party
coffers with the news that Charles Kennedy intends to take back
his empties.

HEALTH
The discovery of a dead swan in Fife led to fears that bird flu had
landed in Britain. The traditional Swan Upping ceremony was
considered inappropriate in the circumstances, and as an additional
precautionary measure Bill Oddie was placed in quarantine.

SPORT
Britain picked up just one medal at the 2006 Winter Olympics.
Shelley Rudman won silver in the women's skeleton, finishing just
ahead of Teri Hatcher, Victoria Beckham and Kate Moss.

There was trouble outside the Frankfurt branch of Asda after Michael Schumacher's wife was accused of parking her car in such a way that everybody behind her had to slow down. 'I couldn't get near the trolleys,' groaned Mrs Kim Raikkonen.

The most unseemly sporting episode of the year occurred in chess, after British grandmaster Danny Gormally took exception to an Armenian rival making a move on beautiful Australian player Arianne Caoili, described as the 'Anna Kournikova of the chess world'. As Levon Aronian danced with Ms Caoili at a party, Gormally, sensing that the Armenian was about to take his queen, marched over and allegedly punched him. It was suggested that Gormally would have got across the dance floor quicker, but then he remembered that he could only move diagonally.

SCIENCE
While walking his dog Dandy on Clapham Common, Mr Eric Petherbury, forty-six, of Station Road, Balham, stumbled across a new planet. The planet, which is believed to have been orbiting Tooting for millions of years, was found behind a hedge. *Blue Peter* viewers were asked to come up with a name for the new planet and 52 per cent chose 'Val' in honour of former presenter Valerie Singleton. London Transport says it hopes to service Val by 2011.

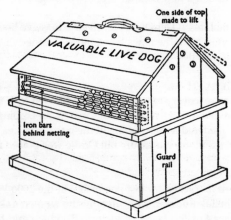

Important features of this box in which to send a small dog by rail are: the sloping roof; bars backed with wire; holes for ventilation; and the guard rail to prevent packages being squeezed against the box and excluding the air.
The contents should always be described on the outside, as shown.

One side of top made to lift

VALUABLE LIVE DOG

Iron bars behind netting

Guard rail

US FASHION DESIGNER MR BLACKWELL'S
WORST DRESSED LIST, 2006

Britney Spears: 'From Princess of Pop to the ultimate Fashion Flop – looks like an over-the-hill Lolita.'

Mary-Kate Olsen: 'Bag lady rags that look depressingly decayed.'

Jessica Simpson: 'It's time to sack the stylist and divorce the designer – she resembles a cut-rate Rapunzel slingin' hash in a Vegas diner.'

Eva Longoria: 'Gorgeous face, garish taste.'

Mariah Carey: 'The world applauds your musical emancipation, but please leave that body to our imagination.'

Paris Hilton: 'Hot? I think not.'

Anna Nicole Smith: 'Queen Kong in cheap lingerie.'

Shakira: 'Coiffure by Medusa, clothes by the Marquis de Sade.'

Lindsay Lohan: 'Drowning in grown-up groaners.'

Renée Zellweger: 'She looks like a painted pumpkin on a pogo stick.'

CATCHPHRASES THAT MIGHT MAKE THE DALEKS
MORE SOCIALLY ACCEPTABLE

Ex-fol-i-ate: destroy the enemy by buying them expensive skin care treatments.

Ex-agg-er-ate: destroy the enemy by means of hyperbole and other linguistic devices.

Ex-as-per-ate: destroy the enemy by irritating them to distraction.

Ex-hil-ar-ate: destroy the enemy by getting them over-excited.

Ex-pat-ri-ate: destroy the enemy by politely asking them to leave their country.

Ex-post-ul-ate: destroy the enemy by means of peaceful protest.

Ex-tra-pol-ate: destroy the enemy by confusing them with mathematical data.

Ex-tort-ion-ate: destroy the enemy by overcharging them.

Ex-certi-fic-ate: destroy the enemy by showing them naughty films.

THE UK'S LEAST DESIRABLE HOLIDAY DESTINATIONS OF 2006

Stoke-on-Trent bus station
Spaghetti Junction
Dogger Bank
Luton Arndale Centre
Watford Gap services
Rotherham KFC
Ratcliffe-on-Soar power station
Gloucester city abattoir
Reading City Council refuse site
The Dartford Tunnel

SOME FAIRLY LONG WORDS

The following were offered by the 2006 *Countdown* champion, fourteen-year-old Conor Travers:

Bresaola: Italian salted-beef fillet.
Craniates: from the Latin *cranium*; animals that have a skull.
Protamine: any of a group of simple proteins found combined with nucleic acids, especially in fish sperm.
Renegado: archaic Spanish term for renegade.
Valorise: to raise or fix the price of a commodity by artificial means, especially by government action.
Ritenuto: musical term meaning an immediate reduction of speed.
Joinder: from the French *joindre*; the act of bringing together.
Diurnal: of or during the day, not nocturnal.
Maidan: an Indian word referring to an open space used as a park or parade ground.
Polonies: Bologna sausages.
Hetairas: courtesans or mistresses in ancient Greece.

2B OR 5C, THAT IS THE QUESTION

In 2006 it was revealed that some British schools were using simplistic GCSE revision guides to make Shakespeare easier to understand. For example:

MACBETH

Shakespeare's version:
Macbeth: Is this a dagger, which I see before me, the handle toward my hand? Come, let me clutch thee. I have thee not, and yet I see thee still show. False face must hide what the false heart doth know.

Revision guide version:
Macbeth: Oooh! Would you look at that.

ROMEO AND JULIET

Shakespeare's version:
Tybalt: What, art thou drawn among these heartless hinds? Turn thee, Benvolio, look upon thy death.

Revision guide version:
Tybalt: Come and have a go if you think you're hard enough.

Shakespeare's version:
Juliet: Good pilgrim, you do wrong your hand too much, which mannerly devotion shows in this; for saints have hands that pilgrims' hands do touch, and palm to palm is holy palmers' kiss.
Romeo: Have not saints lips, and holy palmers too?
Juliet: Ay, pilgrim, lips that they must use in prayer.

Revision guide version:
Juliet: What are you thinking about?
Romeo: Oh, just moons and spoons in June.
Juliet: Wow. Give us a snog then.

A YEAR OF DATES

There were lots of dates in 2006 – 31 January, 9 March, 16 June, 24 August, to name but a few. However, two stood above the crowd like Peter Crouch chaperoning the Seven Dwarfs.

At two minutes and three seconds past 1 a.m. on 4 May, 2006, the time and date in Britain read 01.02.03.04.05.06, the first time this scenario had occurred for 100 years.

Then, on 6 June, the date was 06/06/06, regarded in folklore as the devil's day. Fittingly, horror film fan Suzanne Cooper gave birth to a son that day and decided to call him Damien after the devil child in *The Omen*. However, Angela Dean, mother of a 6 lb 6 oz baby born on 06/06/06, decided not to tempt fate and instead called her son Robbie.

To mark the day, a fight broke out between Goth cinemagoers at the Bentley Bridge Leisure Park in Wednesfield during a screening of the remake of *The Omen*, confirming, if proof were ever needed, that the devil is alive and well in the West Midlands.

The next big date on the calendar will be in seventy-two years when, at 12.34 on 5 June, 2078, it will be 12345678. Don't have nightmares.

LEAST POPULAR GOOGLE SEARCHES, 2006

Ann Widdecombe in leather
Tirana nightclubs
Earwax modelling
Sunnyview Retirement Home nude calendar
Satanism in Godalming
Goldfish wrestling
Dick Cheney Hunting Vacations: accommodation availability

TWELVE BOOKS THAT DIDN'T CHANGE THE WORLD

Rhino Horn Stockpile Management: Minimum Standards and Best Practices from East and Southern Africa – Simon Milledge

Amputation Stumps: Their Care and After-treatment – Sir Godfrey Martin Huggins

Reusing Old Graves – Douglas Davies and Alastair Shaw

The Book of Marmalade: Its Antecedents, Its History and Its Role in the World Today – C. Anne Wilson

Greek Rural Postmen and Their Cancellation Numbers – Anon

Handbook of Surface Treatment and Coatings – Michel Cartier

Penetrating Wagner's Ring – John L. Di Gaetanao

Oral Sadism and the Vegetarian Personality – ed. Glenn C. Ellenbogen

Highlights in the History of Concrete – Christopher Stanley

Development in Dairy Cow Breeding and Management: and New Opportunities to Widen the Uses of Straw – Anon

Versailles: The View from Sweden – Elaine Evans Dee

Ancient Starch Research – Robin Torrence and Huw J. Barton

CHANTELLE: A LIFE MORE ORDINARY

One of the literary events of autumn 2006 was the publication of the autobiography of *Celebrity Big Brother* contestant Chantelle Houghton. Some critics carped that, at twenty-three, she was too young to be writing her autobiography, particularly as her life to date appeared to have been decidedly unremarkable. But as this short extract from her book shows, hers has already been a life rich in drama and excitement:

> I just couldn't believe what was happening to me! It was 7.15 and I'd overslept by five minutes! God, I swear, that had never happened to me before! Bloody amazing! I reckon it was that cheap alarm clock Preston bought – it probably didn't go off or whatever it is they do. But my day was just about to get worse – much worse, scarily worse!! Cos when I went down to the fridge, there was no milk! No bloody milk! Unbelievable! How do these incredible things keep happening to me? What I'd give to lead a normal, boring life. But at times like this you have to be strong, you have to cope with whatever crises life throws at you, and you have to say to yourself: 'I'm going down to the corner shop to get some more milk.' So I did, and on the way (and how spooky is this?) some guy was walking in the opposite direction to me! I felt like a celebrity with a stalker . . . except that he wasn't actually following me. In fact, he jumped on a number 32 bus and I haven't clapped eyes on him since, but it really shook me up at the time. Why does this sort of thing only ever happen to me? I bet nobody can explain it. There's just never a dull moment when I'm around, that's for sure!!!

THE MOST SOCIALLY EXCLUSIVE BRITISH SURNAMES (AS REVEALED IN A 2006 SURVEY)

Fortescue	Pakenham
Goldstein	Pigden
Mukherjee	Cadbury
Pelly	Baring

SOME CURRENCIES OF THE WORLD

Afghanistan
afghani (= 100 puls)
Albania
lek (= 100 qindarka)
Angola
kwanza (= 100 lwei)
Armenia
dram (= 100 luma)
Azerbaijan
manta (= 100 gopik)
Bangladesh
taka (= 100 paisa)
Bhutan
ngultrum (= 100 chetrum)
Bolivia
boliviano (= 100 centavos)
Botswana
pula (= 100 thebe)
Brunei
ringgit (= 100 sen)
Bulgaria
lev (= 100 stotinki)
Costa Rica
colon (= 100 centimos)
Croatia
kuna (= 100 lipas)
Czech Republic
koruna (= 100 haleru)
Ecuador
sucre (= 100 centavos)
Eritrea
nakfa (= 100 cents)
Estonia
kroon (= 100 senti)
Gambia
dalasi (= 100 butut)

Georgia
lari (= 100 tetri)
Ghana
new cedi (= 100 psewas)
Guatemala
quetzal (= 100 centavos)
Guinea
syli (= 100 centimes)
Haiti
gourde (= 100 centimes)
Honduras
lempira (= 100 centavos)
Iceland
krona (= 100 aurar)
Kazakhstan
tenge (= 100 tiyn)
Kyrgyzstan
som (= 100 tyyn)
Latvia
lat (= 100 santims)
Lesotho
loti (= 100 lisente)
Lithuania
litas (= 100 centu)
Macao
pataca (= 100 avos)
Malawi
kwacha (= 100 tambala)
Maldives
rufiyaa (= 100 lari)
Mauritania
ouguiya (= 5 khoums)
Mongolia
tugrik (= 100 mongos)
Mozambique
metical (= 100 centavos)

Nigeria
naira (= 100 kobo)
North Korea
won (= 100 chon)
Oman
rial (= 1,000 baizas)
Panama
balboa (= 100 centesimos)
Papua New Guinea
kina (= 100 toeas)
Paraguay
guarani (= 100 centimos)
Poland
zloty (= 100 groszny)
Qatar
riyal (= 100 dirhams)
Romania
leu (= 100 bani)
Slovakia
koruna (= 100 halierov)
Slovenia
tolar (= 100 stotinov)

Swaziland
lilangeni (= 100 cents)
Tajikistan
somoni (= 100 dirams)
Thailand
baht (= 100 satang)
Tonga
pa'anga (= 100 seniti)
Turkmenistan
manat (= 100 tenga)
Ukraine
hryvnia (= 100 kopiykas)
Uzbekistan
som (= 100 tiyin)
Vietnam
dong (= 100 xu)
Western Samoa
tala (= 100 sene)
Zaire
zaire (= 100 makuta)
Zambia
kwacha (= 100 ngwee)

PHRASES FEATURING ON 'WHATEVERS', ASDA'S RIVAL TO 'LOVE HEARTS'

Minger	Bovvered
Chav	You What?
Mint	Innit
As If	Proper
Respect	Whatever

HIGHEST-EARNING DEAD CELEBRITIES, 2005

Elvis Presley ($45 million per annum)
Charles M. Schulz ($35 million)
John Lennon ($22 million)
Andy Warhol ($16 million)
Theodor 'Dr Seuss' Geisel ($10 million)
Marlon Brando ($9 million)
Marilyn Monroe/J. R. R. Tolkien ($8 million)
George Harrison/Johnny Cash ($7 million)

SOME INSIGNIFICANT SAINTS' DAYS

17 January: Antony the Abbot (patron saint of basket-makers)
20 January: Sebastian (athletes and neighbourhood watch)
22 January: Vincent of Saragossa (vinegar-makers)
29 January: Francis of Sales (authors)
3 February: Blaise (wool-combers and town criers)
4 February: Veronica (laundry workers)
5 February: Agatha (bell-makers and volcanic eruptions)
6 February: Amand (bartenders and Boy Scouts)
9 February: Apollonia (toothache)
7 March: Thomas Aquinas (students)
9 March: Dominic Savio (choirboys and young offenders)
15 March: Louise de Marillac (social workers)
17 March: Joseph of Arimathea (funeral directors)
24 March: Gabriel (postmen)
25 March: Dismas (thieves)
4 April: Ambrose (bee-keepers and wax-melters)
4 April: Isidore (computer programmers)
25 April: Mark (teenagers)
30 April: Adjutor (swimmers)
15 May: Dympna (sleepwalking)
16 May: Honoratus (bakers)
16 May: John Nepomucene (slander)

20 May: Basilissa (chilblains)
20 May: Bernardine of Siena (advertising)
28 May: Bernard of Montjoux (skiers)
29 May: Bona (flight attendants)
2 June: Erasmus (chimney sweeps)
14 June: Basil (hospital administrators)
15 June: Vitus (comedians)
25 June: Eligius (petrol station workers)
25 July: James the Greater (rheumatism)
29 July: Martha (waitresses)
30 July: Abdon and Sennes (barrel-makers)
4 August: Dominic (miscarriages of justice)
12 August: Clare (embroiderers)
13 August: Cassian of Imola (shorthand writers)
18 August: Fiacre (haemorrhoid- and
venereal-disease-sufferers and taxi drivers)
24 August: Bartholomew (Florentine cheese-makers)
25 August: Louis (barbers and button-makers)
28 August: Augustine of Hippo (sore eyes)
8 September: Adrian Nicomedia (arms dealers)
18 September: Joseph of Cupertino (air travellers)
21 September: Matthew (accountants)
27 September: Cosmas and Damian (hairdressers)
29 September: Archangel Michael (shopping)
30 September: Jerome (librarians)
15 October: Teresa of Avila (headaches)
18 October: Luke (butchers)
24 October: Anthony Claret (savings banks)
28 October: Jude (lost causes)
2 November: Eustace (difficult situations)
11 November: Martin (geese)
30 November: Andrew the Apostle (fish dealers)
4 December: Barbara (firework manufacturers)
11 December: Damasus (archaeologists)
13 December: Lucy (haemorrhages)
21 December: Thomas the Apostle (architects)
26 December: Stephen (bricklayers)

MAKES YOU PROUD TO BE BRITISH: A SELECTION OF ENGLAND SONGS FOR THE 2006 WORLD CUP

Baarmy Sheep (with the Cumbria Tourist Board)
– 'Land of Hope and Glory'
Crazy Frog – 'We Are The Champions'
Neil and Christine Hamilton – 'England Are Jolly Dee'
Tony Christie – '(Is This The Way to) The World Cup?'
Sham 69 – 'Hurry Up England'
Stan Boardman – 'Coming Round the Mountain'
The First Eleven with John Cleese – 'Don't Mention the World Cup'
Joe Fagin – 'That's England Alright'
Chris Miller – 'Sven Song'
John Leyton and the Orients – 'Hi Ho Come On England'
Tonedef Allstars featuring Geoff Hurst – 'Who Do You Think You
Are Kidding, Jurgen Klinsmann?'
Jo Babe – 'Tits Out For the Lads'

VAGUELY INTERESTING FACTS ABOUT THE QUEEN THAT EMERGED ON HER EIGHTIETH BIRTHDAY

Since 1952 she has conferred over 387,700 honours and awards.
She has personally held more than 540 investitures.

She has received over three million items of correspondence
during her reign.

She has undertaken 256 official overseas visits to
129 different countries.

Among gifts she has received are jaguars and sloths from Brazil,
two black beavers from Canada, a box of snail shells, a grove of
maple trees and 7 kg of prawns.

She has attended thirty-four Royal Variety performances, opened fifteen bridges and launched twenty-three ships.

She and the Duke of Edinburgh have sent around 37,500 Christmas cards during her reign.

She has given out some 78,000 Christmas puddings to staff.

She has sat for 139 official portraits during her lifetime.

She sent her first email in 1976 from an Army base.

She appeared in a 1941 pantomime, playing Prince Florizel in *Cinderella* in a special performance at Windsor Castle.

She has owned more than thirty corgis and has introduced a new breed, a dorgi, when one of her corgis mated with Princess Margaret's dachshund.

She is patron of the Royal Pigeon Racing Association.

She owns the sturgeons, whales and dolphins in the waters around the UK.

ITEMS LOST ON LONDON'S TRANSPORT SYSTEM, 2006

A 14-foot-long inflatable boat
A jar of bull's sperm
An urn of ashes
Two human skulls in a bag
Three dead bats
A harpoon gun
Glass eyes
A stuffed puffa fish
A DIY vasectomy kit

A coffin
A divan bed
A lawnmower
Breast implants
Two boxes of false teeth
An African mask
False limbs
Three World War Two gasmasks

APRIL FOOL'S JOKES IN THE MEDIA, 2006

The German TV station ZDF reported that the United Nations wants to build a cabled line around the equator.

The Guardian wrote that an alternative to the Chip and PIN card-verification system – Kiss and PIN – is being trialled.

UK radio station 210 FM claimed that an elephant was causing traffic problems on the M4.

Belgian TV station VRT announced that the government would be distributing coupons for a free tanning session in order to help people suffering from spring fatigue caused by the long winter.

The *Daily Mail* stated that Cherie Blair had insisted that the door to 10 Downing Street be repainted red. It also reported that in future apples would be grown with barcodes already on them.

BBC Three Counties Radio told worried listeners that the government was introducing a new car radio licence of £200 a year and that anyone who didn't want to pay it would have to remove their radio from the vehicle.

The Sun reported that a penguin had been spotted in the Thames.

UNSUNG WORLD LEADERS (AS OF JUNE 2006)

Albania: President Alfred Moisiu
Algeria: President Abdelaziz Bouteflika
Angola: President José Eduardo dos Santos
Armenia: President Robert Kocharian
Azerbaijan: President Ilham Aliyev
Bangladesh: President Iajuddin Ahmed
Belarus: President Aleksandr Lukashenko
Benin: President Yayi Boni

Bhutan: King Jigme Singye Wangchuck
Botswana: President Festus Mogae
Burkina Faso: President Blaise Compaoré
Burundi: President Pierre Nkurunziza
Cambodia: King Norodom Sihamoni
Cameroon: President Paul Biya
Cape Verde: President Pedro Pires
Central African Republic: President François Bozizé
Chad: President Idriss Déby
Comoros: President Azali Assoumani
Costa Rica: President Oscar Arias
Cyprus: President Tassos Papadopoulos
Djibouti: President Ismail Omar Guelleh
Dominica: President Nicholas Liverpool
Dominican Republic: President Leonel Fernandez
East Timor: President Xanana Gusmão
Ecuador: President Alfredo Palacio
El Salvador: President Antonio Saca
Equatorial Guinea: President Teodoro Obiang Nguema Mbasogo
Eritrea: President Isaias Afewerki
Estonia: President Arnold Rüütel
Fiji: President Ratu Josefa Iloilo
Finland: President Tarja Halonen
Gabon: President Omar Bongo
Ghana: President John Kufuor
Guinea: President Lansana Conté
Guyana: President Bharrat Jagdeo
Haiti: President René Préval
Honduras: President Manuel Zelaya
Indonesia: President Susilo Bambang Yudhoyono
Kazakhstan: President Nursultan Nazarbayev
Kiribati: President Anote Tong
Kyrgyzstan: President Kurmanbek Bakiyev
Laos: President Khamtai Siphandon
Latvia: President Vaira Vike-Freiberga
Lebanon: President Emile Lahoud
Lesotho: King Letsie III
Lithuania: President Valdas Adamkus

Madagascar: President Marc Ravalomanana
Malawi: President Bingu wa Mutharika
Mauritius: President Sir Anerood Jugnauth
Mongolia: President Nambaryn Enkhbayar
Nauru: President Ludwig Scotty
Panama: President Martin Torrijos
Paraguay: President Nicanor Duarte
Peru: President Alejandro Toledo
Portugal: President Anibal Cavaco Silva
Samoa: Ole Aoole Malo Malietoa Tanumafili II
Senegal: President Abdoulaye Wade
Serbia and Montenegro: President Svetozar Marovic
Seychelles: President James Michel
Sierra Leone: President Ahmad Tejan Kabbah
Slovakia: President Ivan Gasparovic
Slovenia: President Janez Dmovsek
Suriname: President Ronald Venetiaan
Swaziland: King Mswati III
Thailand: King Bhumibol Adulyadej
Tonga: King Taufa'ahau Tupou IV
Uzbekistan: President Islam Karimov
Vanuatu: President Kalkot Mataskelekele
Venezuela: President Hugo Chávez
Yemen: President Ali Abdullah Saleh
Zambia: President Levy Mwanawasa

TOP CELEBRITY ENDORSERS, 2006

Catherine Zeta Jones (T-Mobile) £11.5 million
Angelina Jolie (St John)/Nicole Kidman (Chanel No. 5) £7 million
Jessica Simpson (Guthy-Renker) £4.3 million
Gwyneth Paltrow (Estée Lauder)/Charlize Theron (Dior) £3.4 million
Julia Roberts (Gianfranco Ferré) £3 million
Brad Pitt (Heineken)/Scarlett Johansson (L'Oréal)/
Penelope Cruz (L'Oréal) £2.3 million

UK TOWNS' FAVOURITE GOOGLE SEARCH WORDS

Bradford: Osama bin Laden, Victoria Beckham
St Albans: gym, weight loss
Basildon: sex
Salford: divorce
Liverpool: Armani
Winchester: Hitler, global warming
Brentford: Viagra
London: champagne
Wigan: swinging
Glasgow: whisky
Aberdeen: savings, kebabs
Thames Ditton: hot water bottles, Noel Edmonds
Abingdon: Prince Harry
Gloucester: pig
Milton Keynes: sheds, wigs, Terry Wogan
Norwich: bananas
Edinburgh: *The Da Vinci Code*
Sheffield: speed cameras, *Doctor Who*
Maidenhead: Paul McCartney
Winnersh: flip-flops

CLUB BALL
An olde English game that was probably the origin
of rounders and baseball. As can be seen, it
provided healthy outdoor exercise for the
physically different of the thirteenth century.

WAGS' TALES

For all the excitement of the 2006 World Cup, the real competition took place off the pitch among the England players' wives and girlfriends – or WAGs as they are known collectively. Here's how their performance rated (marks out of ten):

Victoria Beckham
Made her mark from the outset by reportedly arriving in Germany with sixty pairs of sunglasses and jeans in three sizes (in case she lost weight). Had to hire a private jet for £21,000 just to reach the finals, after her scheduled flight was cancelled. Turned out for the opening game in a patriotic outfit of white jeans with a red cross on the pocket and was, as befits her status, the last WAG to board the coach. Still the first choice for most neutrals. **9**

Coleen McLoughlin (Wayne Rooney's girlfriend)
The main pretender to Victoria's crown began well by arriving for her first World Cup with two huge suitcases and two large holdalls. To ensure there were no sartorial blunders, she was said to be consulting her stylist back in England before wearing an outfit in public. She was also reported to have had her own fake-tan therapist in tow. Showed her class by allegedly spending around £600 in a ten-minute German shopping spree and by flying 900 miles home to Liverpool mid-way through the tournament, partly for tactical changes to her hairdo. Clearly a major threat. **8**

Melanie Slade (Theo Walcott's girlfriend)
A shock selection for the tournament, and inexperience showed as she ventured out dressed in High Street clothes and without the obligatory triple-layered varnish of spray-tan. She also arrived with a disappointingly modest amount of luggage. A lot to learn, but time is on her side. **5**

Abigail Clancy (Peter Crouch's girlfriend)
Very blonde and very tanned, she adapted well to her new high-profile role, wearing the most revealing outfit to the Paraguay game and announcing that she was about to relaunch her pop career. Promising debut, but, judging by her T-shirt, could do with more support up front. **6**

Elen Rives (Frank Lampard's girlfriend)
Made an immediate impact by reportedly being thrown off her
flight out to Germany after rowing with Heathrow staff over the
amount of hand baggage she was carrying. Once in Germany, she
was photographed dancing on tables to 'I Will Survive'. A spirited
performance. **7**

Alex Curran (Steven Gerrard's fiancée)
Like Coleen, she flew out her own tan therapist, at a cost of around
£7,500, but was in danger of being substituted after being seen
dining in McDonald's, the last place any self-respecting WAG
would be seen. Apart from that elementary mistake, she slotted
neatly into the side without ever really imposing her presence. **6**

Emma Hadfield (Gary Neville's fiancée)
Was unfashionably first to arrive at the WAGs' hotel and with the
smallest amount of luggage. More was expected from her. **6**

Carly Zucker (Joe Cole's girlfriend)
After a slow start, she began to occupy plenty of column inches.
But being photographed wearing the same cropped top more than
once shows there is still much work to be done if she is to become
an automatic first choice. **7**

Nancy Dell'Olio (Sven-Göran Eriksson's girlfriend)
Sporting the favoured big sunglasses, lashings of fake tan, 'bling'
jewellery and dazzlingly bright clothes, Nancy was never less than
eye-catching. Showed her instinct for a photo opportunity by
sitting next to Prince William at the Paraguay game, but faded
badly as the tournament went on, even committing the cardinal
WAG sin of appearing to shun the limelight. Ultimately, her last
appearance with England was not one to remember. **5**

REASONS WHY VARIOUS LIBERAL DEMOCRATS WERE FORCED TO DROP OUT OF THE 2006 PARTY LEADERSHIP RACE

One was found to have been seeing a rent boy.
Another was found to have been living with a TV weather girl.
Another was revealed as the killer of Bambi's mum.
Another was unmasked as the man who shot Kennedy.
Another admitted he was a James Blunt fan.
Another was discovered to be teetotal.
Another was washing his hair.

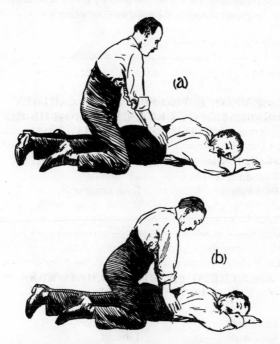

SCHAFER'S METHOD OF ARTIFICIAL RESPIRATION

(a) Place hands on small of patient's back. (b) Thrust forward to force air out of lungs. Then spring back into position (a) to allow the lungs to expand by their own elasticity. Repeat the two operations twelve times a minute until natural breathing recommences or a police officer with a torch appears.

RAZZIES – THE TWENTY-SIXTH ANNUAL GOLDEN RASPBERRY AWARDS

Worst picture: *Dirty Love*
Worst actor: Rob Schneider (*Deuce Bigalow: European Gigolo*)
Worst actress: Jenny McCarthy (*Dirty Love*)
Worst supporting actor: Hayden Christensen
(*Star Wars III: Revenge of the Sith*)
Worst supporting actress: Paris Hilton (*House of Wax*)
Worst screen couple: Will Ferrell and Nicole Kidman (*Bewitched*)
Worst remake or sequel: *Son of the Mask*
Worst screenplay: *Dirty Love,* written by Jenny McCarthy
Worst director: John Asher (*Dirty Love*)

SOME PEOPLE WHO SIR PAUL McCARTNEY PROBABLY DIDN'T GET A CARD FROM ON HIS SIXTY-FOURTH BIRTHDAY

Heather Mills McCartney   Sven-Göran Eriksson
Batman and Robin   Mr Benn
Fred Elliott   John Lennon

UNLUCKIEST PREMIUM BOND TOWNS IN THE UK, 2005

Leicester   Llandudno
Lancaster   Lincoln
Llandrindod Wells   Nottingham
Newcastle upon Tyne   Guildford
Birmingham   Northampton

THE RUDEST CITIES IN THE WORLD
(FROM A 2006 SURVEY)

Mumbai
Bucharest
Kuala Lumpur
Seoul
Moscow/Singapore
Jakarta/Taipei
Ljubljana/Hong Kong
Bangkok
Milan/Sydney
Helsinki/Manila
Amsterdam
London/Paris/Lisbon/Buenos Aires/Johannesburg

FIVE FAVOURITE HOTEL ITEMS FOR
LIGHT-FINGERED BRITS, 2006

Towels (25%)
Ashtrays (15%)
Drinking glasses (11%)
Slippers (10%)
Bathrobes (8%)

In addition, it was revealed that 2.3 million Brits had stolen hotel mirrors, 1.2 million had taken light fittings, 1.1 million had snatched curtains, 900,000 had pilfered door knobs, 450,000 had removed carpets and 200,000 had somehow managed to smuggle hotel beds past reception.

SOME PLACES IN THE WORLD TO AVOID

Arsoli, Italy
Bald Knob, Arkansas
Bastard, Norway
Belcher, New York
Big Beaver, Pennsylvania
Blueballs, Pennsylvania
Bollock, Philippines
Bottom, North Carolina
Brown Willy, Cornwall
Bum, Azerbaijan
Bumbang, Australia
Climax, North Carolina
Clit, Romania
Condom, France
Crap, Albania
Crotch Lake, Ontario
Cuckoo's Knob, Wiltshire
Cum, Nicaragua
Cunt, Turkey
Dick, Colorado
Dikshit, India
Dildo, Newfoundland
Dong Rack, Thailand
Dump, Jamaica
Erect, North Carolina
Fanny, West Virginia

Fucking, Austria
Hooker, Arkansas
Intercourse, Pennsylvania
Knoblick, Arizona
Labia, Belgium
Lickey End, West Midlands
Minge, Lithuania
Muff, Northern Ireland
Poo, India
Probe, Utah
Pussy, France
Semen, Bulgaria
Shaft, Pennsylvania
Shag Island, Indian Ocean
Shit, Iran
Shite Creek, Idaho
Slut, Sweden
Tampon, Réunion
Tit, Algeria
Turdo, Romania
Twatt, Shetlands
Urin, Papua New Guinea
Vagina, Russia
Wank, Germany
Wankers Corner, Oregon
Wet Beaver Creek, Australia

SOME COUNTRIES THAT DON'T SHARE A BORDER WITH SWITZERLAND

Australia
Thailand
Japan

Chile
Angola
Greenland

DISTINCTIVE AMERICAN PLACE NAMES

Aces of Diamonds, Florida
Bald Head, Maine
Ben Hur, Texas
Big Sandy, Wyoming
Boring, Oregon
Disco, Tennessee
Dismal, Tennessee
Eek, Alaska
Embarrass, Minnesota
Fearnot, Pennsylvania
Fifty-Six, Arkansas
Hell, Michigan
Hot Coffee, Mississippi
Jupiter, Florida

Lollipop, Texas
Mars, Pennsylvania
Monkey's Elbow, Kentucky
No Name, Colorado
Normal, Illinois
Odd, West Virginia
Ogle, Kentucky
Okay, Oklahoma
Panic, Pennsylvania
Peculiar, Missouri
Romance, Arkansas
Toad Suck, Arkansas
Uncertain, Texas
Zzyzx, California

ALTERNATIVE ICONS OF ENGLISHNESS

Chavs
Jack the Ripper
The Sinclair C5

Sellafield
Jim Davidson
Judge Jeffreys
Lemmy from Motorhead
Gang culture

The M25
Richard and Judy
'Three Little Fishes'
   by Frankie Howerd
King John
Litter
The Millennium Dome
White stilettos
The Duchess of Cornwall

MORE PROVERBS

Who keeps company with the wolf will learn to howl.
VIETNAMESE PROVERB

You cannot catch a flea with gloves.
ALBANIAN PROVERB

A bandicoot is lovely to his parents; a mule is pretty to its mate.
INDIAN PROVERB

A dog may die from too much walking, but a fool dies from
worrying about someone else's business.
ROMANIAN PROVERB

The river won't get dirty just by the dog's bark.
AFGHAN PROVERB

The one who digs the hole under someone else will fall
in it himself.
CROATIAN PROVERB

He who has scalded himself on milk weeps when he sees a cow.
SPANISH PROVERB

A herring barrel will always smell of herring.
FRENCH PROVERB

When the mouse is full, the flour tastes bitter.
FAROESE PROVERB

It is hard to hunt the hare out of the bush it is not in.
IRISH PROVERB

What good serve candle and glasses if the owl does not
want to see?
DUTCH PROVERB

With patience and spit one gets the mosquito.
GERMAN PROVERB

The bride who doesn't know how to dance says the
floor is slanted.
ARMENIAN PROVERB

When the frog is eating his chillies, why should the lizard sweat?
GHANAIAN PROVERB

He who sowed wind reaps a typhoon.
FILIPINO PROVERB

Fresh pork and new wine kill a man before his time.
ENGLISH PROVERB

The dead do not know the value of white sheets.
HAITIAN PROVERB

He who wins the first hand leaves with only his pants.
CORSICAN PROVERB

A thistle is a fat salad for an ass's mouth.
SCOTTISH PROVERB

One can't spoil porridge with butter.
RUSSIAN PROVERB

In a piranha-infested river, monkeys drink water using a straw.
BRAZILIAN PROVERB

The rabbit has different eyes than the owl.
CYPRIOT PROVERB

Don't let your daughter-in-law eat autumn eggplants.
JAPANESE PROVERB

The fried pigeon will not fly into your mouth.
HUNGARIAN PROVERB

Even a blind squirrel finds a nut once in a while.
SWEDISH PROVERB

A dead elephant cannot be covered by a lotus leaf.
THAI PROVERB

The more you tramp the dunghill the more the dirt rises.
IRISH PROVERB

You don't have to go and paint the eggs of peacocks.
INDIAN PROVERB

Rather a sparrow today than a bustard tomorrow.
HUNGARIAN PROVERB

If you see your neighbour has shaved his beard, you best start
lathering yours.
MEXICAN PROVERB

A humble calf will feed from two mothers.
POLISH PROVERB

Don't let the peasant know how good the cheese with the pears is.
ITALIAN PROVERB

A hungry hen sees herself in a wheat silo.
TURKISH PROVERB

The gentle cat scratches the worst.
ROMANIAN PROVERB

When it is an unlucky phase, the vulture below shits on the
vulture above.
PORTUGUESE PROVERB

If there is someone to haul the fir tree, there shall be no shortage
of those willing to hold a branch to help.
FINNISH PROVERB

A whistling woman and a crowing hen are neither fit for
God nor man.
ENGLISH PROVERB

Flies never visit an egg that has no crack.
CHINESE PROVERB

NAMES FOR FATHER CHRISTMAS AROUND THE WORLD

Chile: Viejo Pascuero (Old Man Christmas)
China: Dun Che Lao Ren (Christmas Old Man)
Finland: Joulupukki
France: Père Noël
Germany: Weihnachtsmann (Christmas Man)
Hawaii: Kanakaloka
Hungary: Mikulas
Italy: Babbo Natale
Japan: Hoteiosho (A God Who Bears Gifts)
Netherlands: Kerstman
Norway: Julenissen (Christmas Gnome)
Poland: Swiety Mikolaj (St Nicholas)
Russia: Ded Moroz (Grandfather Frost)
Sweden: Jultomten (Christmas Brownie)

FASCINATING FACTS ABOUT VEGETABLES

Asparagus was the first frozen food to go on sale in Britain.

Broccoli has a nervous system and experts believe that it feels pain.

The potato belongs to the same family as deadly nightshade.

The ancient Egyptians believed that mixing half an onion with beer foam would keep death at bay.

The Jerusalem artichoke is actually a native of North America.

It takes more calories to eat a stick of celery than the celery itself contains.

When potatoes were first introduced to Europe in the seventeenth century, they were blamed for outbreaks of leprosy and syphilis.

Instead of a gold medal, the ancient Greeks awarded a stick of celery to their sporting champions.

POINTLESS MANAGEMENT-SPEAK PHRASES

Bring to the table
Touch base
To be in the ballpark
Run this by you
Getting all your ducks in a row
Showstopper
Off-line
Singing from the same hymn sheet

Out of the loop
Think outside the box
Ticks in boxes
Bench-marking
No-brainer
Blue-sky thinking
Oven-ready
The view from 10,000 ft

DAVID CAMERON'S CHOICES FOR DESERT ISLAND DISCS

'Tangled Up In Blue' – Bob Dylan
'Ernie (the Fastest Milkman in the West)' – Benny Hill
'Wish You Were Here' – Pink Floyd
'On Wings of Song' – Mendelssohn
'Fake Plastic Trees' – Radiohead
'This Charming Man' – The Smiths
'Perfect Circle' – REM
'All These Things That I've Done' – The Killers

CREATIVE EXCUSES FOR BEING LATE FOR WORK (FROM A 2006 US SURVEY)

'My son tried to flush our ferret down the toilet and I needed to tend to the ferret.'

'I dreamed that I was fired, so I didn't bother to get out of bed.'

'I had to take my cat to the dentist.'

'I went all the way to the office and realized I was still in my pyjamas and had to go home to change.'

'I stopped for a bagel, the store was robbed and the police requested everyone to stay for questioning.'

'A bee flew in my ear and attacked me and I had to pull over.'

'I couldn't find the right tie, so I had to wait for the stores to open so I could buy one.'

'I wet my pants and went home to change.'

'I saw that you weren't in the office, so I went out looking for you.'

'I ran over a goat.'

PLACE NAMES AND THEIR MEANINGS

Acapulco: conquered city
Addis Ababa: new flower
Bangkok: region of olive trees
Beijing: northern capital
Brussels: buildings on a marsh
Canberra: meeting-place
Copenhagen: merchants' harbour
Dublin: black pool
Jakarta: place of victory
Khartoum: end of elephant's trunk
Kuala Lumpur: mouth of the muddy river
Limerick: bare area of ground
Montevideo: I saw the mountain
Rangoon: end of strife
Topeka: a good place to dig potatoes

SOME CATCHY NATIONAL ANTHEMS

Faroe Islands: 'Tú Alfagra Land Mitt'
('O Faroe Islands, My Dearest Treasure')
Honduras: 'Tu Bandera es un Lampo de Cielo'
('Your Flag is a Heavenly Light')
Japan: 'Kimi Ga Yo'
('May a Thousand Years of Happy Reign Be Yours')
Maldives: 'Gavmii Mi Ekuverikan Matii Tibegan Kuriime Salaam'
('In National Unity Do We Salute Our Nation')
Myanmar: 'Kaba Ma Kyei'
('Till the End of the World, Myanmar')
Nepal: 'Rastriya Gaan'
('May Glory Crown You, Courageous Sovereign')
Senegal: 'Pincez Tous vos Koras, Frappez les Balafons'
('Pluck Your Koras, Strike the Balafons')

LOST IN TRANSLATION: BOTCHED ADVERTISING CAMPAIGNS

'Come alive with the Pepsi generation' was translated into Chinese as 'Pepsi brings your ancestors back from the grave'.

General Motors' Chevrolet Nova proved a non-starter in Spain because 'no va' means 'won't go'.

Chicken magnate Frank Perdue's slogan 'It takes a strong man to make a tender chicken' was translated into Spanish as 'It takes an aroused man to make a chicken affectionate'.

Translated into Spanish, the Coors slogan 'Turn it loose' became 'Suffer from diarrhoea'.

Blissfully unaware of the American take on the word 'sucks', Scandinavian vacuum cleaner manufacturer Electrolux gallantly ran a US campaign: 'Nothing sucks like an Electrolux'.

The KFC slogan 'finger-lickin' good' was translated into Chinese as 'eat your fingers off'.

The Ford Pinto car had to be hastily renamed for sale in Brazil after it was discovered that 'pinto' is Brazilian slang for 'tiny male genitals'.

SOME WELSH ROADS

A478   A487   A465   A4112
A4086   B4348   B4415

SOME CELEBRITY PHOBIAS

Oprah Winfrey: chewing gum
Madonna: thunder
Leonardo DiCaprio: cracks in the pavement
Katharine Hepburn: dirty hair
Johnny Depp: spiders, ghosts and clowns
Cameron Diaz: doorknobs
Alfred Hitchcock: eggs
Lyle Lovett: cows
Pamela Anderson: mirrors
Sigmund Freud: ferns
Orlando Bloom: pigs
Sid Caesar: haircuts
Sarah Michelle Gellar: graveyards

Queen Elizabeth I: roses
Gareth Gates: bats
Alexander the Great: cats
Matthew McConaughey: revolving doors
Christina Ricci: ghosts, gerbils, houseplants and selachophobia –
the fear of a shark swimming through a hatch in the side of a
swimming pool.

SOME UNUSUAL PHOBIAS YOU MIGHT LIKE TO TRY

Barophobia: fear of gravity
Clinophobia: fear of going to bed
Pogonophobia: fear of beards
Aulophobia: fear of the flute
Gephyrophobia: fear of crossing bridges
Siderodromophobia: fear of train travel
Ecclesiaphobia: fear of churches
Scoleciphobia: fear of worms
Levophobia: fear of the left side
Genuphobia: fear of knees
Glossophobia: fear of public speaking
Siderophobia: fear of the stars
Ichthyophobia: fear of fish
Trypanophobia: fear of pointed objects
Alektorophobia: fear of chickens
Onomatophobia: fear of certain names
Geniophobia: fear of chins
Ephebiphobia: fear of teenagers
Linonophobia: fear of string
Nephophobia: fear of clouds
Pediophobia: fear of dolls
Triskaidekaphobia: fear of the number thirteen
Paraskavedekatriaphobia: fear of Friday the 13th
Hexakosioihexekontahexaphobia: Fear of the number 666

Curing a chair
that rocks.
A very simple
and quick
operation.

MIND-BOGGLING FACTS ABOUT *TOP OF THE POPS*

The pilot episode was called *The Teen & Twenty Record Club*.

•

One audience member collapsed during the first show, forcing Jimmy Savile to do two links with the man propped up against his legs.

•

Denise Sampey spun the records for the first few shows before being replaced by Samantha Juste, ex-wife of Monkee Mickey Dolenz.

•

When the Rolling Stones made an early appearance, excited teenage fans smuggled their way into BBC Television Centre in the back of a bin lorry.

•

P. J. Proby performed 'Somewhere' with one arm in plaster after being bitten by his dog.

•

Cliff Richard was the show's most regular guest, making over 150 appearances.

•

Alan Freeman introduced 'Cast Your Fate to the Wind' as 'Cast Your Wind to the Fate'.

•

Soul singer R. Kelly demanded forty-three security guards to protect him during his appearance on *Top of the Pops*.

•

When the wrong track was put on, Jimi Hendrix found himself miming to an Alan Price hit. Hendrix muttered: 'I like the voice, man, but I don't know the words.'

•

Fat Les held the record for having the most people on stage when he invited seventy-five others to help sing 'Jerusalem'.

•

Dexy's Midnight Runners played their soul tribute 'Jackie Wilson Said' in front of a huge blow-up of darts player Jocky Wilson.

FORGETTABLE *TOP OF THE POPS* PRESENTERS

Andy Peebles (1981–4)   Dixie Peach (1985–6)
Jenny Powell (1989–90)   Sybil Ruscoe (1989–90)
Simon Parkin (1989–91)   Adrian Rose (1991–3)
Bear Van Beers (1995–6)   Tim Kash (2003)

FOODS THAT HAVEN'T YET BEEN RULED UNSAFE TO EAT

Cabbage   Sardines
Twiglets   Kumquats
Braised vole   Fruit gums (not the green ones)

FAMOUS PEOPLE FROM SWINDON

Billie Piper
Julian Clary
John Francome
David Hempleman-Adams
Mark Lamarr
Desmond Morris
XTC
Diana Dors
Justin Hayward
Gilbert O'Sullivan
Melinda Messenger

THE BOTTOM LINE: SOME FAMOUS PEOPLE WHO SUFFERED FROM PILES

Napoleon
Charles Dickens
Marilyn Monroe
Socrates
Alexander the Great
Anton Chekhov
The Duke of Wellington
Kenneth Williams
King George II
Martin Luther
Edgar Allan Poe
Queen Victoria
Casanova
William Wordsworth

DUMBING DOWN: INSPIRED ANSWERS ON RADIO AND TV QUIZZES

Quizmaster: Name the funny men who once entertained kings and queens at court.
Contestant: Lepers.

Q: What is the capital of Italy?
C: France.

Q: How many wheels are there on a unicycle?
C: Three.

Q: In which European city was the first opera house opened in 1637?
C: Sydney.

Q: What was signed to bring World War I to an end?
C: Magna Carta.

Q: Who wrote *Lord of the Rings*?
C: Enid Blyton.

Q: How long did the Six-Day War between Egypt and Israel last?
C: 14 days.

Q: How many toes would three people have in total?
C: 23.

Q: Name a film starring Bob Hoskins that is also the name of a famous painting by Leonardo da Vinci.
C: *Who Framed Roger Rabbit*.

Q: What is the name of the long-running TV comedy show about pensioners: '*Last of the* . . . '?
C: Mohicans.

Q: What happened in Dallas on 22 November, 1963?
C: I don't know, I wasn't watching it then.

Q: How many kings of England have been called Henry?
C: Well, I know there was Henry the Eighth. Er, three?

SOME *CORONATION STREET* CHARACTERS WHO HAVE DIED OF HEART ATTACKS

May Hardman, 1960
Martha Longhurst, 1964
Jack Walker, 1970
Cyril Turpin, 1974
Jerry Booth, 1975
Derek Wilton, 1997
Billy Williams, 1997
Des Barnes, 1998
Alf Roberts, 1999
Mike Baldwin, 2006

LITTLE-KNOWN CLOUD TYPES

Arcus: thick, arch-shaped cloud with ragged edges, usually attached to cumuli.
Intortus: curved and tangled cirrus.
Opacus: a dense, shadowy sheet of cloud.
Lacunosus: a thin cloud with holes and ragged edges.
Velum: like a ship's sail in appearance.
Pileus: hood-shaped cumulus-type cloud.
Perlucidus: a sheet of cloud with small holes.
Tuba: a trumpet-like column hanging from the base of cumuli.
Translucidus: a translucent sheet of cloud.
Vertebratus: cirrus arranged in such a way that it looks like the bones of a skeleton.
Duplicatus: double, partly merged, layers of cloud.
Incus: anvil-shaped cloud.
Radiatus: parallel lines converging at a central point, often cirrus.
Pannus: shredded sections attached to the main cloud.
Undulatus: wavy cloud with an undulating pattern.

FREAK SPORTING INJURIES

Baseball player John Smoltz burned his chest while ironing a
shirt he was wearing.

•

Former Chelsea goalkeeper Dave Beasant missed the start of the
1993-4 season after dropping a jar of salad cream on his big toe.

•

England cricketer Derek Pringle injured his back while
writing a letter.

•

US boxer Daniel Caruso broke his own nose while psyching
himself up for a fight by pounding his gloves into his face.

•

New Zealand rugby player Howard Joseph was injured in 1971
after tripping over a boxer dog that had strayed on to the pitch.

•

Liverpool striker Robbie Fowler suffered a knee injury by
stretching to pick up the TV remote control.

•

Weightlifter Mike Tereui damaged a hand while punching a pig
that was raiding his vegetable patch.

•

Dorset golfer Derek Gatley knocked himself out with his own
backswing when the club shaft snapped.

•

Scottish sprinter Euan Clarke missed a number of races in 1991
after cutting his eyeball while trying to wipe sweat from his
forehead with a crisp packet.

•

Boxer Adolpho Washington missed out on the WBA light-
heavyweight title in 1993 after a TV cameraman left him with a
badly cut eye. Washington had already sustained eye damage from
opponent Virgil Hill, but when the cameraman moved in for a
close-up of the injury between rounds he accidentally banged the
wound with his camera. Suddenly Washington started to bleed
profusely and had to retire.

Nantwich Town footballer Andy Kinsey dislocated his shoulder throwing his shirt to the crowd after scoring his team's third goal in the 2006 FA Vase final.

•

Celebrating his country's surprise 1967 Davis Cup victory over the United States, Ecuador captain Danny Carrera made a mess of trying to jump the net and broke his ankle.

•

Baseball player Wade Boggs hurt his back when he lost his balance while trying to put on cowboy boots.

•

Sunderland footballer Kevin Kyle scalded his privates with boiling water while feeding his young son.

•

Yorkshire and England cricketer Chris Old damaged a rib as a result of a violent sneeze.

•

French rugby player Jean-Pierre Salut broke his ankle after tripping on the stairs leading from the dressing-room to the pitch.

•

Golfer John Morgan was bitten by a rat while addressing his ball on the tenth fairway at the 1968 Open at Carnoustie.

•

Snooker player Stephen Lee was forced to withdraw from the 1999 British Open after twisting a neck muscle while answering the phone.

•

Baseball player Kevin Mitchell strained a muscle while vomiting.

•

Cricketer Nigel Briers sprained his thumb after catching it in his trouser pocket.

SEQUELS THAT SHOULD NEVER HAVE BEEN MADE

Jaws 2   *Grace and Favour*   George W. Bush

COUNTRIES THAT HAVE SCORED *NUL POINTS* IN THE EUROVISION SONG CONTEST

Austria, 1962 (Eleonore Schwartz: 'Nur in Der Wiener Luft')
Belgium, 1962 (Fud Leclerc: 'Tom Nom')
Netherlands, 1962 (De Spelbrekers: 'Katinka')
Spain, 1962 (Victor Balaguer: 'Llamame')
Finland, 1963 (Laila Halme: 'Muistojeni Laulu')
Netherlands, 1963 (Annie Palmen: 'Een Speeldoos')
Norway, 1963 (Anita Thallang: 'Sohlverv')
Sweden, 1963 (Monica Zetterlund: 'En Gang I Stockholm')
Germany, 1964 (Nora Nova: 'Mann Gewohnt Sich So Schnell An Das Schone')
Portugal, 1964 (Antonio Calvario: 'Oracao')
Switzerland, 1964 (Anita Traversi: 'I Mei Pinsieri')
Yugoslavia, 1964 (Sabahudin Kuri: 'Zivot Sklopio De Skrug')
Belgium, 1965 (Lize Marke: 'Alles Het Weer Lente Is')
Finland, 1965 (Viktor Klimenko: 'Aurinko Laskee Lanteen')
Germany, 1965 (Ulla Weisner: 'Paradies, Wo Bist Du?')
Spain, 1965 (Conchita Bautista: 'Que Bueno, Que Bueno')
Italy, 1966 (Domenico Mudugno: 'Dio Come Ti Amo')
Monaco, 1966 (Tereza: 'Bien Plus Fort')
Switzerland, 1967 (Geraldine: 'Quel Cor Vas-tu Briser?')
Luxembourg, 1970 (David Alexandre Winter: 'Je Suis Tombé Du Ciel')
Norway, 1978 (Jahn Teigen: 'Mil Etter Mil')
Norway, 1981 (Finn Kalvik: 'Aldri i Livet')
Finland, 1982: (Kojo: 'Nuku Pommiin')
Spain, 1983 (Remedios: 'Quien Maneja Mi')
Turkey, 1983 (Cetin Alp and Short Wave: 'Opera')
Turkey, 1987 (Seyyal Tanner and Locomotif: 'Sarkim Sevgi Usgune')
Austria, 1988 (Wilfried: 'Lisa, Mona Lisa')
Iceland, 1989 (Daniel: 'Pad Sem Enginn Ser')
Austria, 1991 (Thomas Forstner: 'Venedig im Regen')
Lithuania, 1994 (Ovidius Vysnianskas: 'Lopisine Mylimaj')
Norway, 1997 (Tor Endreson: 'San Francisco')
Portugal, 1997 (Celia Lawson: 'Antes de Adeus')
Switzerland, 1998 (Gunvor: 'Lass Hin')
United Kingdom, 2003 (Jemini: 'Cry Baby')

SOME PEOPLE'S HEIGHTS (AS OF JUNE 2006)

Roman Abramovich: 6 ft 2 in
J.K. Rowling: 5 ft 4 in
Queen Elizabeth II: 5 ft 3 in
Sir Alan Sugar: 5 ft 7 in
Anne Robinson: 5 ft 1 in
Sir Mick Jagger: 5 ft 10 in
Barbara Windsor: 4 ft 11 in
Peter Crouch: 6 ft 7 in
Simon Cowell: 5 ft 9 in
Tom Cruise: 5 ft 7 in
Elle Macpherson: 6 ft
Keira Knightley: 5 ft 7 in

FILMS THAT ARE JUST WAITING TO BE MADE

Harry Potter and the Rubber-clad Dominatrix
Lassie the Kitten Killer
Superman Comes Out
Bambi: The Venison Years
Bridget Jones Tops Herself
Wallace & Gromit: Plasticine Meltdown

SOME BALLET POSITIONS

Devant	Glissade	Pas	Pas de chat
Pas de deux	Pas jeté	Relevé	Rond de jambe

ACCEPTED INDICATIONS THAT YOU'VE REACHED THE AGE OF THIRTY

You leave clubs before the end 'to beat the rush'.

Before going out anywhere, you ask what the parking is like.

When sitting outside a pub, you become envious of their hanging baskets.

Before throwing the newspaper away, you look through the property section.

You buy your first T-shirt without anything written on it.

You always have enough milk in the house.

Instead of throwing out an old pair of trainers, you keep them because they might be good for the garden.

You are unable to resist the lure of self-assembly furniture.

You find yourself saying, 'Is it cold in here or is it just me?'

Instead of tutting at old people who are slow getting off the bus, you tut at schoolchildren's lousy grammar.

You wish you had a shed.

You have a shed.

BRITISH CREATURES THAT YOU DO NOT SEE AS MUCH AS YOU USED TO

House sparrow   Song thrush   Water vole   Postman

GOOD SCRABBLE WORDS

Oryx: an Arabian antelope
Xyster: a surgeon's instrument
Qanat: an irrigation tunnel
Xebec: a sailing boat
Zouk: a style of popular music with a heavy Caribbean influence
Xeme: a fork-tailed gull
Xylem: plant tissue
Zebu: a humped ox
Xylic: a kind of acid
Qibli: a warm wind
Qanon: a dulcimer-like instrument
Zax: a slater's chopper

A SELECTION OF FRENCH CHEESES

Abondance: a semi-hard, fragrant cheese from Savoie.
Broccui: a white cheese made from ewe's milk and produced on the island of Corsica.
Carré de l'Est: a cheese from Lorraine, with a smoky-bacon flavour.
Chaource: creamy and crumbly with a white rind, it is manufactured in the Champagne region.
Époisses: from Côte d'Or, it is pungent and orange-coloured and is sold in a circular wooden box.
Livarot: a soft, pungent cheese from Normandy.
Morbier: creamy with a black seam through the middle, it hails from Franche-Comté.
Reblochon: a soft, creamy cheese with a nutty flavour from Savoie.
Saint-Nectare: a silky texture with a subtle taste of hazelnut and mushrooms, from Auvergne.

DAYS OF THE *VENDÉMIAIRE*, THE FRENCH REPUBLICAN CALENDAR (22 SEPTEMBER–21 OCTOBER)

Raisin (grape)
Safran (saffron)
Châtaigne (chestnut)
Colchique (crocus)
Cheval (horse)
Balsamine (impatiens)
Carotte (carrot)
Amaranthe (amaranth)
Panais (parsnip)
Cuve (vat)
Pomme de terre (potato)
Immortelle (strawflower)
Potiron (squash)
Réséda (mignonette)
Âne (donkey)

Belle de nuit (a type of flower)
Citrouille (pumpkin)
Sarrasin (buckwheat)
Tournesol (sunflower)
Pressoir (wine-press)
Chanvre (hemp)
Pêche (peach)
Navet (turnip)
Amaryllis
Boeuf (beef)
Aubergine
Piment (chilli pepper)
Tomate (tomato)
Orge (barley)
Tonneau (barrel)

SOME ENEMIES THAT DOCTOR WHO HAS YET TO ENCOUNTER

Big Issue sellers
Wheel clampers
The Young Conservatives
Market researchers
Double-glazing salesmen
Jehovah's Witnesses
Footballers' agents
The paparazzi
Sharon Osbourne

AN A–Z OF SONG TITLES FEATURING GIRLS' NAMES (EXCEPT FOR THE TRICKY ONES)

'Angie' – The Rolling Stones
'Barbara Ann' – The Beach Boys
'Oh Carol' – Neil Sedaka
'Debora' – T. Rex
'Come On Eileen' – Dexy's Midnight Runners
'Frankie and Johnny' – Elvis Presley
'Georgy Girl' – The Seekers
'Helen Wheels' – Paul McCartney
'Poison Ivy' – The Coasters
'Juliet' – The Four Pennies
'Kayleigh' – Marillion
'Tell Laura I Love Her' – Ricky Valance
'Mary' – Scissor Sisters
'Nadine (Is It You)' – Chuck Berry
'Ophelia' – Natalie Merchant
'Pamela Pamela' – Wayne Fontana
'Ruby Don't Take Your Love to Town' – Kenny Rogers
'Sorry Suzanne' – The Hollies
'Tammy' – Debbie Reynolds
'Ursula (the Swansea Song)' – Barclay James Harvest
'Valerie' – The Zutons
'Wendy Clear' – Blink 182
'The Ballad of John and Yoko' – The Beatles
'Zoe' – Paganini Traxx

INDIAN EMPERORS (AD 320–550)

Chandragupta I (320–50)
Chandragupta II (376–415)
Skandagupta (455–70)
Budhagupta (475–500)
Narasimhagupta (515–30)
Vishnugupta (540–50)

Samudragupta (350–76)
Kumaragupta I (415–55)
Kumaragupta II (470–5)
Vainyagupta (500–15)
Kumaragupta III (530–40)

FAMOUS BRANDS THAT ARE NO LONGER BRITISH

Harry Ramsden's: sold to Swedish-owned EQT in 2006.

The Body Shop: sold to L'Oréal of France in 2006.

Manchester United: sold to US tycoon Malcolm Glazer in 2005.

HP Sauce: sold to US firm Heinz in 2005.

Ty-phoo Tea: sold to the Apeejay Surrendra Group of India in 2005.

Weetabix: sold to US firm Hicks, Muse, Tate & Furst in 2003.

Hamleys: sold to Icelandic retail group Baugur in 2003.

Fortnum & Mason: sold to Whittington Investments of Canada in 2001.

Oxo: sold to American conglomerate Campbell's in 2001.

Bentley: sold to Germany's Volkswagen in 1998.

The Mini: sold to German car manufacturer BMW in 1994.

Tetley's Bitter: sold to Danish brewer Carlsberg in 1991.

Rowntree: sold to Swiss firm Nestlé in 1988.

SUBTERRANEAN RIVERS OF LONDON

Moselle	Walbrook	Fleet
Tyburn	Effra	Neckinger
Bloo Brook	Stamford Brook	Counter's Creek

LAPSED OLYMPIC SPORTS

Hangman: Last took place at the 1992 Barcelona Olympics where, in a dramatic conclusion to the celebrity word section, the French team's entry of 'Ruby Wax' was pipped for the gold medal by Hungary's 'Lulu'.

Origami: At the 1928 Amsterdam Olympics, Scottish origami experts Ken Pugh and Donald McDonald ripped the opposition to shreds by making a scale model of the Forth Road Bridge from an old copy of the *Daily Mail* in just under three-and-a-half minutes. Reigning champions Mexico could manage only bronze with a paper bracelet.

Bingo: Few who were present will ever forget the climax to the bingo competition at the 1964 Tokyo Olympics where the host nation yelled 'house' a split-second before the USSR team. The Soviets claimed that the Japanese player had his hand up before the international caller had finished saying the number – a clear contravention of the rules – but their appeal was overruled and the incident led to diplomatic relations being broken off between the two countries for three-and-a-half years.

Tiddlywinks: Olympic tiddlywinks was last seen at the 1976 Montreal Games. The UK was the hot favourite until a finger injury sidelined its star flicker, Kevin Scrunge. Without him, it had to settle for silver behind the Dutch, whose free-flowing, avant-garde 'total tiddlywinks' revolutionized the sport.

Mowing the lawn: With the 1956 Olympics being held in Melbourne during what is widely accepted as being the golden age of Australian lawn-mowing, it came as little surprise when the host nation's perfect parallel lines earned it gold. But there were accusations of home bias after American hopes were shattered by moles.

Battleships: At the insistence of the Germans, Battleships was included in the 1936 Olympics, but in a shock result that left the watching Hitler apoplectic with rage, the last German cruiser was sunk by the Swiss team. Hitler's fury was such that the sport was immediately banned in Germany and any mention of the decisive squares – A8, A9 and A10 – became a capital offence.

Twisting balloons into funny shapes: To the surprise of some, this sport earned Olympic status at the 1924 Games in Paris where, thanks in no small part to the efforts of Henri Chimbaud (aka M. Twisti-Twosti), France picked up no fewer than three gold medals. After his instant giraffe had the judges purring with delight in the individual animal section (scoring maximum marks for both artistic impression and technical merit), he helped Ballon Équipe Français to further golds in the team freestyle and team discipline events. The competition was marred when the Romanian entrant inhaled prematurely and was last seen floating over Lille.

Binge-drinking: A controversial inclusion for the 2000 Sydney Olympics at the instigation of the home nation, the binge-drinking competition proved a disaster for the UK team whose abject failure led to its members being roundly booed when they arrived back at Heathrow stone-cold sober. The appointment of Charlotte Church as performance director raised hopes for the future, but the event was dropped for the Athens Games amid fears that drunken competitors might find the local women attractive.

Wallpapering: Although sixteen countries sent the cream of the world's hangers to the wallpapering competition at the 1952 Helsinki Olympics, it boiled down to a straight fight for gold between Mexico and Norway. The Mexicans were on course for victory until they lost valuable time negotiating that tricky little bit in the corner around the light socket.

Sheep worrying: It came as no great surprise that New Zealand took gold when this event was staged at the 1956 Melbourne Olympics. Once again the British failed miserably: their sheep didn't look at all worried and were so relaxed they were even seen partying on the town the night before their heat.

Happy Families: A popular inclusion at the 1912 Stockholm Olympics, Happy Families produced a thrilling finale, with Italy snatching gold by revealing the precise whereabouts of Mr Bun the Baker. The scenes of wild celebration, which saw members of the

Italian party jumping fully clothed into the Baltic, were soured by Belgian protests that Mrs Chop the Butcher's Wife was missing from the pack. Then the Moroccans complained that the Italians had defaced Master Sole the Fishmonger's Son by drawing on a false moustache to confuse their rivals. It all turned very ugly and although Italy was allowed to keep the gold medal, Happy Families was dropped from future Olympics.

ACRONYMS TO REMEMBER

BISEPS: Battlefield Identification System Environment Performance Simulation
CASTOR: Canadian Automatic Small Telescopes for Orbital Research
CLEMARS: California Law Enforcement Mutual Aid Radio System
ENTEC: Euro NATO Training Engineer Centre
FEAST: Forum for European-Australian Science and Technology
FONSI: Finding Of No Significant Impact
GLAAD: Gay and Lesbian Alliance Against Defamation
HIMEZ: High Altitude Missile Engagement Zone
IMRI: Industrial Membrane Research Institute
KIDS: Knowledge-based Integrated Data System
NUDIS: Nuclear Detonation Information Summary
SEDRIS: Synthetic Environment Data Representation and Interchange Specification
SMART: Subject Matter and Requirements Team
SNAP: Supernova Acceleration Probe
TUNS: Technical University of Nova Scotia
VERITAS: Very Energetic Radiation Imaging Telescope Array System
WHAM: Wisconsin Hydrogen-alpha Mapping

BRITISH SITCOMS' US TITLES

Are You Being Served? became *Beane's of Boston*
Birds of a Feather became *Stand By Your Man*
Dad's Army became *Rear Guard*
Fawlty Towers became *Snavely*
The Likely Lads became *Stuebenville*
Mind Your Language became *What a Country!*
On the Buses became *Lotsa Luck*
Rising Damp became *27 Joy Street*

Also:
Absolutely Fabulous became *Totally Hysterical* in Sweden
The Vicar of Dibley became *The Vicar in Stilettos* in Poland
Steptoe and Son became *Albert Og Herbert* in Sweden
Fawlty Towers became *Tall John's Inn* in Finland

THINGS THAT HAPPEN EVERY YEAR AT WIMBLEDON

All the British women are knocked out by the first Wednesday
(unless it has rained for a day).
•
It rains.
•
Sir Cliff Richard is seen in the crowd.
•
Experts ask, 'Can this finally be Tim Henman's year?'
•
Lots of people go 'Ooooh'.
•
Lots of people go 'Aaaah'.
•
Men who hate tennis suddenly taken a keen interest in matches
featuring Russian girls.
•
Somebody yells, 'Come on Tim' even after Henman has just lost.
•
Sue Barker produces a long list of excuses as to why British players
failed yet again.

REWRITTEN WORKS OF LITERATURE

How Green Was My Valet – the moving story of a naïve Welsh butler

•

Great Expectorations – a practical guide to advanced coughing

•

The Merry Chavs of Windsor – pram-pushing teenagers talk about life
in the Home Counties

•

Lady Chatterley's Plover – an aristocratic siren shows her tender side
by taking a sea bird under her wing

•

Trulliver's Gavels – auctioneer Ernest Trulliver reveals the secrets of
the trade in this entertaining memoir

•

Le Mallard Imaginaire – a French hypochondriac is haunted by an
imaginary duck

•

Under Milk Tray – a sad tale about a box of Terry's All Gold that
finds itself at the bottom of the supermarket shelf

•

The War of the Wolds – a disturbing novel chronicling the bitter
rivalries between several Lincolnshire villages

•

The Wind in the Pillows – the tense story of a husband who has to
apologize to his wife after eating Brussels sprouts in bed

•

Of Meissen Men – porcelain figures come to life when the antiques
shop shuts for the night

•

For Whom the Tell Bowls – a fourteenth-century Swiss folk hero
takes up cricket to defeat the Austrian enemy

CHEAP AT HALF THE PRICE

In 1993 Oxford butcher Mike Feller paid £990 for a 101-year-old joint of ham.

A bucket of manure from a British Olympic gold medal horse fetched £760 on eBay in 2004.

A piece of Britney Spears's used chewing gum sold on eBay for £10,000.

The red slippers worn by Judy Garland in *The Wizard of Oz* fetched £90,000 at auction in 1988.

The body tag from the corpse of Lee Harvey Oswald, John F. Kennedy's assassin, sold for £3,600 at auction.

In 2006 retired Hampshire taxi driver John Clarke sold two pairs of 1969 Marks & Spencer string underpants and a matching string vest to collectors in London and Hong Kong for £273 on eBay.

Joni Rimm paid £35,000 to charity in return for a forty-five-second snog with Sharon Stone in 2003.

A collection of 2,000 glass eyeballs sold for £20,125 at Sotheby's in 1998.

A mouldy biscuit from the launch of the *Titanic* was sold for £3,525 in 2001.

A pair of Bryan Adams's dirty socks sold for £551 on eBay.

The loin cloth that Charlton Heston wore in the movie *Ben Hur* fetched £6,250 in 1997.

In 1988 a Gloucestershire bookseller paid £3,575 for a lock of Lord Nelson's hair.

A bottle of Lake District air – described as 'the perfect accompaniment' to the cultural offerings of William Wordsworth – sold on eBay for £60 in 2004.

A 1965 letter written by John Lennon to his then-wife Cynthia was sold for £17,250 in 1997.

A nineteenth-century vampire-killing kit was sold for £2,500 on eBay.

A nightcap believed to have been worn by Charles I at his 1649 execution was sold for £13,000 at Christie's in 1983.

Justin Timberlake's half-eaten French toast (complete with fork and syrup) sold for £2,000 on eBay.

The supposedly lucky phone number 8888-8888 was bought by China's Sichuan Airlines for £188,000 in 2003.

A hanging plastic fern from Elvis Presley's Graceland home sold for £395 on eBay.

One of Sir Isaac Newton's teeth was sold for £730 in 1816, to a nobleman who had it set in a ring.

Newsreader Kate Garraway's half-eaten banana fetched £1,650 on eBay.

A card, handwritten by J.K. Rowling and bearing ninety-three words of clues to the contents of *Harry Potter and the Order of the Phoenix*, sold for £28,000 in 2002.

In 2005 Sasha Gardner posted the following item for sale on eBay: 'A small yellow bucket containing a scoop of seawater from Bournemouth beach (left of the pier). The bucket has a handle and there are no stones in the water but a thin layer of sand occupies the bottom.' Within a week a London man had paid £50 for it.

RELIGIOUS ITEMS BOUGHT BY GOLDEN PALACE ONLINE CASINO

The Virgin Mary Grilled Cheese Sandwich, bought from a Florida woman for £16,000 in 2004.

•

An image of the Virgin of Guadalupe in a Texas tree was bought for £3,000 in 2006.

•

'Shower Jesus', a bathroom water stain supposedly bearing the image of Jesus, was bought for £1,100 from a Pittsburgh man in 2005.

•

A vegetable pie bearing the face of Jesus was bought from an Ohio family for £1,000 in 2005.

•

The Divine Pretzel – a honey-mustard pretzel depicting the Virgin Mary holding baby Jesus – was bought from a Nebraska family for £650 in 2005.

•

A piece of sheet metal showing the image of Jesus was bought from a Connecticut man for £850 in 2006.

•

A Doritos chip in the shape of the Pope's mitre was bought for £700 from a Massachusetts man in 2005.

•

An Xbox bearing Jesus's face was bought for £300 in 2006.

•

A chicken breast resembling Pope John Paul II was bought for £160.

•

An Ontario apartment door featuring an image of Mother Teresa was bought for £150 in 2005.

•

An image of the Virgin Mary (in hooded cloak) in an unborn baby's sonogram was bought from a California mother for £75.

•

An Australian man's frying pan featuring a likeness of Jesus in burned leftover lemon-mustard cream sauce was bought for £60.

•

A Cheeto corn snack in the shape of the Baby Jesus wrapped in swaddling clothes was bought from a Seattle family for £15 in 2005.

SOME SONGS WITH FRUIT IN THE TITLE

'Blackberry Way'
'Pineapple Head'
'Cherry Oh Baby'
'Little Green Apples'
'Raspberry Beret'
'Clementine'
'Orange Crush'
'Strawberry Fields Forever'
'Banana Boat Song'
'Blueberry Hill'
'Peaches'
'I Heard It Through the Grapevine'

OXYMORONS

Fun run	Sweet sorrow
Peace force	Beginning Finnish
Working holiday	Military intelligence
Crash landing	Old news
Head butt	Virtual reality
Rap music	Pretty ugly
Business ethics	Microsoft Works

SOME HANDY NUMBERS TO KNOW
BETWEEN 1 AND 20

6   19   4   7   11   3

EXCUSES GIVEN BY BEATEN BRITISH PLAYERS AT WIMBLEDON

'The grass was too long.'
'The grass was too short.'
'The grass was too green.'
'The white lines gave me a headache.'
'I was a haddock in a previous life, so I didn't want to get too near the net.'
'I wanted to get home to watch *Countdown*.'
'I don't really like tennis.'

SOME (ALLEGEDLY) GAY RULERS

Elagabalus of Rome (217–22)
William II of England (1087–1100)
Richard I of England (1189–99)
Edward II of England (1307–27)
John II of France (1350–64)
James III of Scotland (1469–88)
Henri III of France (1574–89)
James I of England (1603–25)
Louis XIII of France (1610–43)
Mary II of England (1688–94)
William III of England (1689–1702)
Anne of England (1702–14)
Gian Gastone de' Medici, Grand Duke of Tuscany (1723–37)
Gustav III of Sweden (1771–92)
Louis XVIII of France (1814–24)
Ludwig II of Bavaria (1864–86)
Otto I of Bavaria (1886–1913)
Ferdinand I of Bulgaria (1908–18)

UNCOMMON BRITISH PUB NAMES

The Cheese and Chunder
The Weapons of Mass Destruction
The Nag's Husband
The Nice Cup of Tea and a Biscuit
The Queen's Liver
The Sheep Shagger
The Chief Constable
The Adder's Arms
The Arsonist
The Thieving Landlord
The Mary Whitehouse

ANAGRAMS

Dormitory – dirty room
Desperation – a rope ends it
The Morse Code – here come dots
Slot machines – coins lost in 'em
Mother-in-law – woman Hitler
Eleven plus two – twelve plus one
Evangelist – evil's agent
William Shakespeare – I am a weakfish speller
The Conservative Party Conference – French contraceptives on
every seat
Justin Timberlake – I'm a jerk, but listen
Arnold Schwarzenegger – he's grown large 'n' crazed
Jennifer Aniston – fine in torn jeans
Sharon Stone – no near shots
President Clinton of the USA – to copulate he finds interns

AMBASSADOR TO THE WORLD: THE DUKE OF EDINBURGH'S FINEST INSULTS

Chatting with British students in China in 1986, he warned them: 'If you stay here much longer you'll go back with slitty eyes.'

•

In 1993 he told a Briton living in Hungary: 'You can't have been here long. You've not got a pot belly.'

•

On a state visit to Canada, he snapped at an official: 'We don't come here for our health, you know.'

•

He once asked his Italian hosts if they knew what the smallest book in the world was, and then told them it was the *Book of Italian Heroes*.

•

In 1998 he said to a student who had trekked through Papua New Guinea: 'So you managed not to get eaten then?'

•

He once upset the French by saying: 'Isn't it a pity Louis XVI was sent to the guillotine?'

•

On a trip to Panama, he shouted at his police escort who had sounded a siren: 'Switch that bloody thing off, you silly fucker!'

•

In 1999 while touring a Scottish factory, he commented that a fuse box 'looked as though it had been put in by an Indian'. (Buckingham Palace was forced to issue an apology.)

•

In 2002 during a tour of Australia, he asked the founder of an Aboriginal cultural park: 'Do you still throw spears at each other?'

SOCIETIES YOU MAY CARE TO JOIN

Flotation Tank Association

National Toothpick Holder Collectors' Society

Bagpipe Society

Dental History Society

American Association of Aardvark Aficionados

Sausage Appreciation Society

Boomerang Society

Flat Earth Society

Extreme Ironing Bureau

World Rock Paper Scissors Society

Jim Smith Society (membership open only to people called Jim Smith)

International Brick Collectors' Association

International Society of Skateboarding Moms

George Formby Society

Procrastinators Club of America

Wallpaper History Society

National Button Society

Bus Enthusiasts Society

Maledicta Society (for those who enjoy swearing)

Cheese Club

Test-Card Circle

Richard III Appreciation Society

Cheirological Society

Vacuum Cleaner Collectors' Club

YET MORE PROVERBS

When it is raining porridge, the beggars have no spoons.
IRISH PROVERB

Not only did the monkey ruin himself, he also ruined the garden.
INDIAN PROVERB

They catch up with a liar sooner than a limping dog.
HUNGARIAN PROVERB

You can't make a piano out of a bacon box.
IRISH PROVERB

The peg is greater than the stake.
INDONESIAN PROVERB

Who fears the sparrows must not sow millet.
TURKISH PROVERB

So often goes the cat to the fat that she loses her paw.
ITALIAN PROVERB

The chicken that cries at night will not lay eggs in the morning.
ALBANIAN PROVERB

The hole is more honourable than the patch.
IRISH PROVERB

Grabbing excrement is better than grabbing flatulence.
THAI PROVERB

The last shirt has no pockets.
GERMAN PROVERB

It's a cracked pitcher that goes longest to the well.
ENGLISH PROVERB

Every frog must know its sole-leather.
BULGARIAN PROVERB

God does not give horns to a cow that likes to gore.
RUSSIAN PROVERB

One searches for someone else's donkey while singing songs.
TURKISH PROVERB

No matter how long the procession, it still ends up in church.
FILIPINO PROVERB

The spit of the toad doesn't reach the white dove.
FRENCH PROVERB

Only the shoe knows the stocking to be torn.
POLISH PROVERB

God gives nuts to he who has no teeth.
PORTUGUESE PROVERB

Every fisherman loves best the trout that is of his own tickling.
SCOTTISH PROVERB

The nice apples are always eaten by nasty pigs.
BULGARIAN PROVERB

The second boiled broth is always the best.
IRISH PROVERB

He who's born a donkey can't die as a horse.
ITALIAN PROVERB

Water drips from the roof will eventually go to the reservoir.
INDONESIAN PROVERB

One Indian less, one extra tortilla.
HONDURAN PROVERB

When the woman gets off the wagon, horses have an
easier time.
POLISH PROVERB

Don't strike the hot iron with a wooden hammer.
ALBANIAN PROVERB

Seven nurses and the baby has no eyes.
RUSSIAN PROVERB

One shouldn't sell the bear's fur before it has been killed.
GERMAN PROVERB

Little snakes need to grow in hiding.
HAITIAN PROVERB

When a mad man throws a stone in the water, ten wise men
can't get it out.
ROMANIAN PROVERB

If your wife wants to throw you off the roof, try to find
a low one.
SPANISH PROVERB

You don't miss the cow until the stall is empty.
SWEDISH PROVERB

Small pots have big ears.
DUTCH PROVERB

Never say die when there is meat on the shin of a wren.
IRISH PROVERB

SOME TYPES OF EEL

Moray	Worm	Arrowtooth
False moray	Snipe	Snubnosed
Conger	Witch	Sawtooth
Longneck	Snake	Electric
Cutthroat	Jellied	Platform

THINGS YOU PROBABLY DIDN'T KNOW ABOUT BRITAIN

Ten per cent of Britons mention their pet in their will.

Around 80,000 umbrellas are lost
annually on the London Underground.

William the Conqueror ordered that
everyone should go to bed at eight
o'clock.

There are more than 30,000 John Smiths
living in Britain.

As Britain originally lived by the Julian
calendar, until 1752 New Year's Day fell
on 25 March.

In the sixteenth century it was legal for husbands to beat their
wives – but not after 10 p.m.

The British take 2,793,000 tins of baked beans on holiday with them
each year.

In 1945 a flock of starlings landed on the minute hand of Big Ben
and put the time back by five minutes.

In the nineteenth century anyone in Britain who tried to commit
suicide and failed was hanged.

Nowhere in Britain is more than seventy-four-and-a-half miles from
the sea.

Fifty per cent of Britons take their own sweets to the cinema.

The town of Beverley, near Hull, was named after the beavers that
once lived in the region.

SCOTTISH FILMS

Look Back in Angus

Renfrew Over the Cuckoo's Nest

Nightmare on Sauchiehall Street

The Blair Atholl Project

A Starry Sporran

Thelma and Lulu

Romancing the Stonehaven

Alloa Dolly

Fiddler on the Social

Close Encounters of the Thurso Kind

Yankee Doodle Dundee

You've Got Crail

Hawicker Man

When Harry Lauder Met Sally

Meet Me in St Andrews

My Fair Laddie

A Pish Called Wanda

Dunbar and Dunbar

Dances with Swords

Haggis Who's Coming to Dinner

Journey to the Centre of Perth

The Grapes of Rothesay

Vanishing Pint

Poor Cow . . . Denbeath

Bairn Free

Forfar from the Madding Crowd

An American Werewolf in Lochgelly

Honey, I've Sold the Kids

WELSH FILMS

The Magnificent Severn

The Wizard of Oswestry

Dai Hard

Cool Hand Look – You

Dial M For Merthyr

Haverfordwest Was Won

The Bridge on the River Wye

Lawrence of Llandybie

Independence Dai

A Fish Called Rhondda

Seven Brides from Seven Sisters

The Welsh Patient

Breakfast at Taffynys

Evans Can Wait

9¹/₂ Leeks

NATIONAL SUPERSTITIONS

In Slovenia, if you dream about money you will get lice.

In France, it's bad luck to cross a stream while carrying a cat.

In Germany, it is thought that if a dog runs between a woman's legs,
her husband will beat her.

In Italy, you must touch iron immediately after seeing a nun
in order to avoid bad luck.

In Poland, bringing lilac into the house is a sign of impending death.

In Spain, it is considered bad luck to leave a bed unmade
on 1 November.

In Japan, it is unlucky to pick up a comb with its teeth facing you.

In Nigeria, a man struck with a broom becomes impotent unless he
retaliates seven times with the same broom.

In Russia, it's unlucky to pick up something immediately
after you've dropped it.

In Greece, it is bad luck to put your shoes down with the
soles facing up.

In Romania, anyone who takes salt in their hand on Easter Day
will have sweaty hands all year.

In Germany, it is believed that rainwater found on tombstones
will remove freckles.

In Holland, people with red hair are thought to bring bad luck.

In Hungary, if a woman sits at the corner of a table, she will
never get married.

In Italy, hearing a cat sneeze brings good fortune.

In Scotland, the sight of three swans flying together means a national disaster is imminent.

In France, it is apparently good luck to tread in dog poo with your left foot.

RESTRICTED JUNCTIONS ON THE M56

Junction 1: Westbound: no exit. Access only from M60 (westbound). Eastbound: no access. Exit only to M60 (eastbound) & A34 (northbound).

Junction 2: Westbound: no access. Exit only to A560. Eastbound: no exit. Access only from A560.

Junction 3: Westbound: no exit. Access only from A5103. Eastbound: no access. Exit only to A5103 & A560.

Junction 4: Westbound: no access. Exit only. Eastbound: no exit. Access only.

Junction 9: Westbound: Exit to M6 (southbound) via A50 interchange. Eastbound: Access from M6 (northbound) via A50 interchange.

Junction 15: Westbound: no access. Exit only to M53. Eastbound: no exit. Access only from M53.

CAPITAL OFFENCES IN THE UK IN THE NINETEENTH CENTURY

Being in the company of gypsies for one month

Defacing Westminster Bridge

Cutting down a young tree

Stealing goods worth 5s

Setting fire to a haystack

Damaging a fish pond

Writing a threatening letter

Appearing on the highway with a sooty face

Forging the Ace of Spades
(to avoid Stamp Tax on a pack of playing cards)

Impersonating a Chelsea Pensioner

SOME BBC PROGRAMMES THAT VIEWERS MISSED IN THE FIRST WEEK OF WORLD WAR TWO

Beatrice Lillie at the Piano (Monday 4 September 1939)
Down on the Farm (Wednesday 6 September)
Style at Home – 'Bettie Cameron Smail will explain and illustrate
how to achieve the professional touch in home dressmaking'
(Wednesday 6 September)
Ken Johnson and his West Indian Dance Orchestra
(Thursday 7 September)
Blood Donors – a twenty-minute film about giving blood
(Friday 8 September)

PHRASES TO LEARN

Harlez-vous Français? – Do you drive a French motorcycle?

Posh Mortem – Death styles of the rich and famous.

Veni, Vipi, Vici – I came, I'm a very important person, I conquered.

Gott in Rimmel! – What the hell's happened to your makeup?

Haste Cuisine – French fast food.

Respondez S'Il Vous Plaid – Answer if you're Scottish.

Que Sera Serf – Life is feudal.

Zit Alors! – My God, what a pimple!

Quip Pro Quo – A fast retort.

Idios Amigos – We're wild, crazy guys.

Déjà Fu – the feeling that somehow, somewhere, you've been kicked in the head like this before.

Visa La France – Don't leave your château without it.

Monage à Trois – I am three years old.

IMPRESSIVE ART MOVEMENTS

Nabis	Cubism	Fauvism
Dada	Orphism	Neo-Plasticism
Nazarenes	Rayonnism	Abstract Expressionism
Constructivism	Pointillism	Mannerism

THE NEARLY MEN OF HISTORY

Neville Eckersley: History records that in 1522 Portuguese navigator Ferdinand Magellan became the first person to sail around the world. But in fact Yorkshire explorer Neville Eckersley was over 200 miles ahead of Magellan's crew and would have completed his circumnavigation a month earlier than them had he not stopped off at Bordeaux on the way home to buy a present for his wife.

•

Aethelrug Wolfstan: A resident of southern England in the sixth millennium BC, Wolfstan invented the wheel at least 1,000 years before the Mesopotamians. Unfortunately, he had no real idea what to do with his invention and used it as a plant holder.

•

Keith Patterson: Scotsman Patterson and his wife were on a sailing holiday in the Atlantic in 1490 when they discovered America – two years before Columbus. But unable to find any shops open, they quickly left and didn't bother mentioning it to anyone when they got home.

•

Norman Parsons: He was Isaac Newton's next-door neighbour in the 1680s and was sitting in his garden one day when apples from Newton's overhanging fruit tree came crashing down on his head. Leaning over the fence, he complained bitterly to Newton who immediately rushed indoors to write the law of gravity.

•

Fritz Schinken: In 1911, with England's Captain Scott and Norway's Roald Amundsen racing each other for the distinction of becoming the first person to reach the South Pole, a little German, Fritz Schinken, should have beaten both. Leading a two-person expedition, he was three months ahead of the rival parties crossing Antarctica until he decided to let his wife Frida do the map-reading. The Schinkens were never seen again.

SOME PEOPLE WHO MISSED BEING
ON THE *TITANIC*

J. Pierpont Morgan, the owner of the *Titanic*, pulled out at the last minute citing ill health.

Robert Bacon, the outgoing American Ambassador in Paris, cancelled his journey following a phone call from Morgan. His official excuse was that he had to remain in Paris to smooth the way for his successor.

Henry C. Frick cancelled his booking after his wife sprained her ankle.

Frank Adelman caught a later ship after his wife experienced a premonition of impending doom.

George W. Vanderbilt cancelled because his mother-in-law harboured grave reservations about maiden voyages.

James V. O'Brien was delayed by a court case in Ireland.

Rev J. Stuart Holden withdrew on the eve of sailing because his wife was ill.

Edward W. Bill switched to the *Mauretania* after his wife had an alarming dream.

Brothers Bertram, Tom and Alfred Slade had been employed as crew members but missed the ship's departure from Southampton after being held up at a level crossing by a slow-moving goods train.

Harry Burrows was also due to serve on the *Titanic* but, after setting off for Southampton, he suddenly changed his mind and returned home.

PARLIAMO PLYMOUTH – A CONCISE DEVON DIALECT DICTIONARY

appledrane – wasp
back-ze-vore – back-to-front
belve – to sing loudly
bladder – blister
cledgy – sticky
crowder – violinist
crumpdiddy – awkward
dimpsy – twilight
drangway – alley
drexil – doorstep
frawzy – treat
fuz pig – hedgehog
grockle – visitor
heable – pitchfork
jonick – pleasant
kickshaw – entertainment
leary – hungry

lousterin' – hard work
maunderin' – grumbling
mizmaized – confused
mommet – scarecrow
mump aided – silly
oozle – throat
pusky – short of breath
raimid – stretched
slammick – untidy
smitcher – frying pan
taffity – fussy (about food)
thurdle gutted – thin
tizzick – unwell
vauchin – move fast
vitty – alright
zamzodden – stupid
zwant – soft

Key steps in making a tasselled mat.

(a)   *(b)*   *(c)*

ECCENTRIC MUSEUMS

Museum of Dirt, Boston, Massachusetts
Museum of Menstruation, Maryland
Frog Museum, Switzerland
Museum of Barbed Wire, Kansas
German Hygiene Museum, Dresden
Mr Ed's Elephant Museum, Pennsylvania
American Sanitary Plumbing Museum, Massachusetts
National Museum of Pasta Foods, Rome
Carrot Museum, Belgium
European Asparagus Museum, Schrobenhausen, Germany
Mt. Horeb Mustard Museum, Wisconsin
Gourd Museum, North Carolina
Museum of Mazes, Ross-on-Wye
Museum of the Cultural History of the Hand, Wolznach, Germany
Barney Smith's Toilet Museum, Texas
Mini Cake Museum, California
Cockroach Hall of Fame, Texas
International Esperanto Museum, Austria
British Lawnmower Museum, Southport
National Museum of Funeral History, Houston, Texas
Piggy Bank Museum, Amsterdam
Mustard Museum, Dijon, France
Cuckooland Museum, Cheshire
Washington Banana Museum
The Liberace Museum, Nevada
Dog Collar Museum, Leeds Castle, Kent
Museum of Bad Art, Boston, Massachusetts
National Lighter Museum, Oklahoma
Bowling Ball Art Museum, Florida
Leila's Hair Museum, Missouri
Burnt Food Museum, Arlington, Massachusetts
Glore Psychiatric Museum, Missouri
Museum of the Mousetrap, Newport, Wales
The Children's Garbage Museum of Southwest Connecticut

SOME ONLINE MUSEUMS

Incredible World of Navel Fluff
Museum of Odd Socks
Toaster Museum
Bathtub Art Museum
Mel's Fastener Museum
Martin's Owl Collection
Toast Portraits of Famous People
Museum of Coathangers
Dr Darren's World of Crabs

JAPANESE FORMULA ONE DRIVERS, PAST AND PRESENT

Masahiro Hasemi	Kazuyoshi Hoshino
Yuji Ide	Taki Inoue
Ukyo Katayama	Masami Kuwashima
Satoru Nakajima	Shinji Nakano
Hideki Noda	Takuma Sato
Aguri Suzuki	Toshio Suzuki
Toranosuke Takagi	Noritake Takahara
Kunimitsu Takahashi	Sakon Yamamoto

POPULAR TYPES OF HAMMER

Ball-peen	Bush	Claw
Framing	Gavel	Mallet
Maul	Sledge	Stonemason's

FAMOUS PEOPLE WHO HAVE HAD ROSES NAMED AFTER THEM

Dolly Parton
Thora Hird
Abraham Lincoln
Susan Hampshire
John F. Kennedy
Princess Diana
Henry Fonda
Abraham Darby
Sue Lawley
Chevy Chase
Anna Ford
Ingrid Bergman
Paul Smith
Horatio Nelson
Angela Rippon
Christian Dior
Maureen Lipman
Lucille Ball
John Mills
Felicity Kendal

SOME NEW ROSE VARIETIES FOR 2007

Ulrika Jonsson ('an excellent bedder')
George W. ('a low-growing bush but can be invasive')
Monty Panesar ('has a tendency to drop')
Jeremy Paxman ('prickly')
Natasha Kaplinsky ('a determined climber')
Faria Alam ('good against a wall')

FAMOUS TREVORS

Sir Trevor McDonald
Trevor Nelson
Sir Trevor Brooking
Clever Trevor (Ian Dury & the Blockheads)
Trevor and Simon
Sir Trevor Nunn
Trevor the Baptist (John's little-known understudy)

GENUINE QUESTIONS ASKED OF
TELEPHONE OPERATORS

CALLER: I'd like the number of the Argoed Fish Bar in Cardiff, please.
OPERATOR: I'm sorry, there's no such listing. Are you sure you have the spelling correct?
CALLER: Well, it used to be the Bargoed Fish Bar but the B fell off.

CALLER: I'd like the number of the Scottish knitwear company in Woven.
OPERATOR: I can't find a town called Woven. Are you sure you've got the right name?
CALLER: Yes. That's what it says on the label – Woven in Scotland.

CALLER: I'd like the RSPCA please.
OPERATOR: Where are you calling from?
CALLER: The living room.

CALLER: I'd like the number for a reverend in Cardiff, please.
OPERATOR: Do you have his name?
CALLER: No, but he has a dog named Ben.

CALLER: The Union of Shopkeepers and Alligators, please.
OPERATOR: You mean the Amalgamated Union of Shopkeepers?
CALLER: Er, yes.

SOME RECENT ADDITIONS TO THE OXFORD ENGLISH DICTIONARY

Bahookie: n., *Scottish*, a person's buttocks.

Celebutante: n., a celebrity who is well known in fashionable society.

Crunk: n., a type of hip-hop or rap music characterized by repeated shouted catchphrases.

Hoodie: n., a person, especially a youth, wearing a hooded top.

Mentee: n., a person who is advised, trained or counselled by a mentor.

Obesogenic: adj., tending to cause obesity.

Plank: n., *British informal*, a stupid person.

Radge: n., *Scottish informal*, a wild, crazy or violent person.

Upskill: v., to teach an employee additional skills.

ROMAN TOWN NAMES

Aquae Sulis – Bath
Ardotalia – Glossop
Calcaria – Tadcaster
Calleva Atrebatum – Silchester
Camulodunum – Colchester
Cantabria – Cambridge
Corinium – Cirencester
Dubris – Dover
Durnovaria – Dorchester
Durocobrivis – Dunstable
Durocornovium – Swindon
Hortonium – Halifax
Isca Dumnoniorum – Exeter
Lactodorum – Towcester
Noviomagus – Chichester
Ratae Coritanorum – Leicester
Venta Belgarum – Winchester

IN EXCESS: HOW ROCK STARS SPLASH THE CASH

Bono spent £1,000 to have his favourite hat flown first-class from Heathrow to Italy.

•

Elton John lavished £250,000 on flowers between January 1996 and September 1997.

•

When Eric Clapton fell in love with a totem pole during a tour of the United States, he had it flown home and erected in the grounds of his Surrey mansion.

•

At a cost of over £7,000, John Lennon once bought out an entire first-class airline cabin so that his son Sean could play with his model train set.

•

Soccer fan Noel Gallagher spent £20,000 on a carpet in Manchester City's colours.

•

Rod Stewart spent £54,000 on having a full-size football pitch (complete with dressing-rooms) installed in the grounds of his Epping mansion.

•

Donna Summer's birthday cake once travelled first-class on a plane.

•

For a 2003 Mediterranean holiday, rapper P. Diddy rented a 181-ft luxury yacht at a cost of £21,640 per day.

•

Ardent conservationist Sting spent £6,485 on a special living Christmas tree in 2002.

TEN MOST POPULAR US DOG NAMES
TRANSLATED INTO HAWAIIAN

Ua-lohe-ke-Akua (Sam)   Ka Nui (Max)
Haku Wahine (Lady)   Pe'a (Bear)
Momi (Maggie)   Pilialoha (Buddy)
La Hanau (Tasha)   Keleki (Chelsea)
Pomaika'I (Holly)   Na'ena'e (Shasta)

THE WACKY RACERS

Dick Dastardly and Muttley in the Mean Machine
The Gruesome Twosome in the Creepy Coupe
The Slag Brothers in the Bouldermobile
Penelope Pitstop in the Compact Pussycat
Red Max in the Crimson Haybailer
Sarge and Meekley in the Army Surplus Special
Professor Pat Pending in the Convert-A-Car
The Ant Hill Mob in the Roaring Plenty
Peter Perfect in the Varoom Roadster
Rufus Ruffcut and Sawtooth in the Buzz Wagon
Luke and Blubber in the Arkansas Chugga-Bug

ANCIENT ROMAN MEASURES

4 cochlearia = 1 cyathus
12 cyathi = 1 sextarius*
6 sextarii = 1 congius
8 congii = 1 amphora
20 amphorae = 1 culleus

*a sextarius was roughly equivalent to a pint

A CATALOGUE OF SPORTING BLUNDERS

En route to his international rugby debut for France against Scotland in 1911, Gaston Vareilles decided to hop off the team train at Lyon for a sandwich. But he had to queue so long at the station buffet that the train pulled away without him. He missed the match and was never selected again.

•

Arriving in Montreal for the 1976 Olympics, the Czech cycling team's hopes were dashed when all their wheels and spare tyres were accidentally picked up by garbage collectors and crushed.

•

The 1966 Jamaican national track championships were delayed because the organizers had forgotten to bring the starting pistol.

•

Voted Leicester City's 1995–6 Player of the Year for his safe hands, goalkeeper Kevin Poole was presented with a cut-glass rose bowl . . . which he promptly dropped.

•

Having arrived at Worcester racecourse for a 1994 meeting with time to spare, jockey Graham Bradley took a nap in his car. Alas, he overslept and missed the first race. To add insult to injury, the horse he should have ridden, Macedonas, went on to win partnered by Bradley's replacement, Simon McNeill.

•

After being not out against Surrey at the Oval in 1921, Leicestershire cricketer Thomas Sidwell was unable to resume his innings the following morning because he got lost on the London Underground.

•

Callers to a freephone number advertising a US amateur golf tournament in 2000 were alarmed to hear instead a sultry female voice informing them they had 'come to the right place for nasty talk with big-busted girls'.

Driving out from the McLaren garage to the starting grid for the 1999 Australian Grand Prix, Mika Hakkinen was oblivious to the fact that the air-line was still attached to the car. The oversight caused a gantry to be pulled down on to the head of team boss Ron Dennis.

•

Inept marshalling at the 1988 Liege-Bastogne-Liege cycle race sent the entire field of 200 riders speeding down a hill straight into roadworks. More than fifty competitors were brought down in the ensuing pile-up.

•

At the 1991 World Student Games, New Zealand gymnast Raewyn Jack had points deducted after her leotard rode up too high during her exercise.

•

In 1989 Twyford Cricket Club near Bristol staged a special match to bring in urgently needed funds for ground maintenance. It raised £44, but during the match a window was broken by a six and the club had to pay £45 for repairs.

•

In the match-day programme for the 1980 rugby international between France and Ireland, the surname of Irish back row Colm Tucker was spelt with an F instead of a T.

•

Setting off from Scotland at the start of the 1956 Monte Carlo Rally, Dr Alex Mitchell had only travelled 200 yards when he ploughed into a Glasgow Corporation bus.

•

In 1965 an East German junior footballer was sent off for flirting with the referee. The official, twenty-year-old Marita Rall, ordered him off when he tried to arrange a date with her during the match.

•

At the start of a French soccer match in 1950 one of the captains inadvertently swallowed the five-franc piece that the referee was tossing for choice of ends.

CLUEDO ALIASES FOR MRS PEACOCK

Mme Pervenche (France)
Baronin von Porz (Germany)
Capitano Azurro (Switzerland)
Signora Pavone (Italy)
Sra. De Corte-Real (Portugal)
Profesora Rubio (Spain)
Ka. Pagoni (Greece)
Fru Blå (Sweden, Finland, Denmark)
Baronesse von Blauw (Norway)
Sra. Pavorreal (USA – Spanish rules)
Dona Violeta (Brazil)

RELIABLE INDICATORS THAT YOU HAVE CHOSEN A 'NO FRILLS' AIRLINE

Before the flight, the passengers get together and elect a pilot.

You can't board the plane unless you have the exact change.

They don't sell tickets, they sell chances.

All the insurance machines in the terminal are sold out.

Before you take off, the stewardess tells you to fasten your Velcro.

The captain asks the passengers to chip in for fuel.

All the planes have both a bathroom and a chapel.

There's no need for an in-flight movie because your life keeps flashing before your eyes.

SOME VENTRILOQUISTS AND THEIR DUMMIES

Ray Alan (Lord Charles)
Edgar Bergen (Charlie McCarthy)
Peter Brough (Archie Andrews)
Terry Hall (Lenny the Lion)
Keith Harris (Orville)
Neville King (Old Boy)
Shari Lewis (Lamb Chop)
Ronn Lucas (Scorch the Dragon)
Fred Russell (Coster Joe)
David Strassman (Chuck Wood)
Kenny Warren (Leroy Cool)
Arthur Worsley (Charlie Brown)

SOME ISLANDS IN THE THAMES

Lot's Ait
Eel Pie Island
Steven's Eyot
Tagg's Island
Platt's Eyot
Wheatley's Ait
Pharaoh's Island
White Lily Island
Isle of the Great Crostini
Kat Isle
Davage Ait

Glover's Island
Trowlock Island
Raven's Ait
Garrick's Ait
Swan's Rest Island
D'Oyly Carte Island
Truss's Island
Katie-Jo's Island
Poodle Island
Scuttle Island
Isle of Dogs

COMMON SIZES OF BRUSH

$1/8$ in	$1/4$ in	$3/8$ in	$1/2$ in	$5/8$ in	$3/4$ in
$7/8$ in	1 in	$1^1/4$ in	$1^1/2$ in	2 in	$2^1/2$ in
3 in	$3^1/2$ in	4 in			

UNFORTUNATE DEATHS OF RECENT TIMES

American poacher Marino Malerba shot a stag standing proudly above him on an overhanging rock . . . but was killed instantly when the dead stag fell on him.

•

A motorcyclist in South Dakota was fatally hit by an airborne toilet which had apparently fallen off a passing truck.

•

Salvatore Chirilino was walking along the cliff top at Vibo Marina, Italy, when he picked up a four-leaf clover. Just as he was congratulating himself on his good fortune, his foot slipped on the wet grass and he fell over the cliff edge, plunging 150 feet to his death.

•

An eighteen-year-old Arkansas man drowned when he accidentally fell into a water-filled pit while trying to drown his dog, which he thought was too old. The teenager's father also drowned when he jumped in to save his son. The dog survived.

•

A man in Kitwe, Zambia, was electrocuted when, with no space left on his clothes line, he decided to hang the remainder of his wet washing on a live power line that passed his house.

•

A New York construction worker was buried up to his neck after a trench collapsed. Before the emergency crews arrived, a co-worker tried to dig him out with a shovel but accidentally decapitated him.

•

A thirty-seven-year-old man escaped a fire in his South Carolina home, only to die of smoke inhalation after deciding to go back inside to look for his mobile phone so that he could call the fire brigade.

•

Mourners at the funeral of Anna Bochinsky were startled to see the 'dead' woman jump out of her coffin while, as is the custom in Romania, it was being carried to the grave with the lid open. She ran straight into the road, where she was run over and killed by a car.

FACTS THAT YOU REALLY SHOULD KNOW

Tooth fairies dispense £108 million a year.

Nine per cent of men would prefer to give up sex for a week
than give up the TV remote control.

Eighty per cent of head lice are resistant to treatment.

We hit our lowest ebb at 2.16 p.m. each day.

Fathers do £13,000 worth of unpaid jobs for their families
each year.

Humans share 99 per cent of their DNA with chimpanzees.

A cow produces an average of 70,000 glasses of milk in
her lifetime.

Forty per cent of men don't understand how bras undo.

SOME SUBURBS OF BRISBANE

Bald Hills	Coorparoo
Doolandella	Enoggera
Fig Tree Pocket	Indooroopilly
Jamboree Heights	Jindalee
Nudgee	Tarragindi
Toowong	Woolloongabba
Wooloowin	Yeerongpilly

IMAGINATIVE TOWN TWINNING

Birmingham and Milan, Italy
Glasgow and Havana, Cuba
Dundee and Dubai, United Arab Emirates
Darlington and Amiens, France
Doncaster and Wilmington, North Carolina
Chesterfield and Tsumeb, Namibia
Aberdeen and Bulawayo, Zimbabwe
Coventry and Kingston, Jamaica
Leeds and Durban, South Africa
Salford and Narbonne, France
Peterborough and Forli, Italy
Nottingham and Ljubljana, Slovenia
Bournemouth and Netanya, Israel
Bristol and Beira, Mozambique
Bury and Angoulême, France
Hull and Freetown, Sierra Leone

NATIONS WHO HAVE WON MISS WORLD

India (5)
United Kingdom (5)
Venezuela (5)
Iceland (3)
Jamaica (3)
Sweden (3)
Argentina (2)
Australia (2)
Austria (2)
Germany (2)
Netherlands (2)
Peru (2)
South Africa (2)
United States (2)
Bermuda (1)
Brazil (1)
Dominican Republic (1)
Egypt (1)
Finland (1)
France (1)
Greece (1)
Grenada (1)
Guam (1)
Ireland (1)
Israel (1)
Nigeria (1)
Poland (1)
Puerto Rico (1)
Russia (1)
Trinidad & Tobago (1)
Turkey (1)

FORGOTTEN CHARACTERS FROM *NEIGHBOURS*

Phoebe Bright: Oddball, snake-loving teenager who dated Josh Anderson then fell in love with Todd Landers. He got her pregnant, but died after being hit by a van. She married Stephen Gottlieb on the rebound.

Dorothy Burke: The stern principal of Erinsborough High School preferred the company of her pupils after her first husband Colin was imprisoned for fraud. Then, in 1993, she met school inspector Tom Merrick and left Ramsay Street on the back of his motorbike.

Gloria Gardner: Loud-mouthed widow barmaid at the Waterhole. Married Rob Lewis, but he was killed in a car crash after rowing with son-in-law Paul Robinson over stolen garage parts. A distraught Gloria moved to Tasmania.

Mark Gottlieb: Brother of Stephen and Serendipity ('Ren'). He jilted Annalise Hartman at the altar and decided to enter the priesthood instead. Later left to become a TV chef in Sydney.

Jane Harris: The school nerd until she had a makeover and became one of the hottest girls on Ramsay Street. She dated Mike Young and then had a brief fling with Des Clarke, but called off her engagement to him when her grandmother, Nell Mangel, was taken ill.

Julie Martin: Scheming wife of Philip Martin, daughter of Jim Robinson, stepmother of Debbie and Michael and mother of Hannah. Died when she fell off a tower during a murder mystery weekend.

Lance Wilkinson: Studious, somewhat gauche, son of Ruth and twin brother of Anne. After dating Amy Greenwood, he met fellow sci-fi freak Alana and went off with her to live in the United States.

Cody Willis: Tempestuous daughter of Pam and Doug and sister to Adam, Brad and Gaby. Dated, among others, Rick Alessi, 'Stonefish' Rebecchi and Sam Kratz. Shot by drug dealers in 1996 and died a week later.

THE WORLD OF LADDERS
(AND RELATED STRUCTURES)

Extension ladders
Combination ladders
Stepladders
Aluminium platforms
Fibreglass steps
Timber stepladders
Telescopic ladders
Loft ladders
Escape ladders

Surveyors' ladders
Scaffold systems
Warehouse steps
Staging and trestles
Specialist ladders
Step stools
Universal ladders
Roof ladders

REALLY STUPID AIRCRAFT NAMES

Wildebeest (Vickers)
Grebe (Gloster)
Desford (Reid & Sigrist)
Brabazon (Bristol)
Cuckoo (Sopwith)
Camel (Sopwith)
Vernon (Vickers)
Baby (Sopwith)
Parasol (Morane-Saulnier)
Horsa (Airspeed)
Buffalo (Brewster)
Tabloid (Sopwith)
Bullet (Bristol)

SOME LONDON UNDERGROUND STATIONS THAT HAVE CHANGED THEIR NAMES

Surrey Docks (Deptford Road until 1911)
Debden (Chigwell Lane until 1949)
Acton Town (Mill Hill Park until 1910)
Oakwood (Enfield West until 1934)
Arsenal (Gillespie Road until 1932)
Lambeth North (Westminster Bridge Road until 1917)
Warren Street (Euston Road until 1908)
Fulham Broadway (Walham Green until 1952)
Marylebone (Great Central until 1917)
Monument (Eastcheap until 1884)
Barbican (Aldersgate until 1968)
Green Park (Dover Street until 1933)
Moor Park (Sandy Lodge until 1923)

MAGAZINES FOR THE MORE DISCERNING READER

Refractive Eye News
Fertilizer Focus
Pest Control News
Cranes Today
Hooked on Crochet!
Reinforced Plastics
Batteries International
Practical Poultry
Noise and Vibration Worldwide

Concrete Construction
Fish Friers Review
The Rabbit Habit
Coin Slot International
Biscuit World
Linedancer Magazine
Teddy Bear Scene
Rubber Stamp Madness
Cross Stitch Crazy

TOP CAT CHARACTERS

Top Cat   Benny the Ball   Brains   Spook
Choo-Choo   Fancy   Officer Dibble

THE SIX STEPS IN HOME WINEMAKING

Extract flavour from fruit or vegetable.

Add sugar and yeast and ferment for up to ten days in a tightly covered bowl at about 70°F (21°C).

Strain off, put into fermentation jar or bottle. Fit air-lock. Fill to bottom of neck. Allow to complete fermentation at temperature of 60°F (16°C).

Rack the cleared wine. Repeat this about two months later, and often a third time.

Bottle when wine is about six months old. Store bottles on their sides in a room of 55°F (13°C) temperature or below.

Drink.

METRES IN LATIN VERSE

Dactylic Hexameter
Dactylic Pentameter
Iambic Senarius
Iambic Septenarius
Iambic Octonarius
Trochaic Septenarius
Trochaic Octonarius

Hendecasyllabic
Asclepiad
Glyconic
Pherecratic
Alcaic Stanza
Sapphic Stanza

SOME PEOPLE WITH THREE NAMES

Sarah Michelle Gellar
Jamie Lee Curtis
Billy Bob Thornton
Gordon the Gopher

Sarah Jessica Parker
John Selwyn Gummer
Long John Baldry
Anna Nicole Smith

SEPARATED AT BIRTH: UNLIKELY PAIRS BORN ON THE SAME DAY

Dickie Bird and Jayne Mansfield (19 April 1933)

Eric Idle and John Major (29 March 1943)

Roger Taylor of Queen and Thaksin Shinawatra, Prime Minister of Thailand (26 July 1949)

Ben Kingsley and John Denver (31 December 1943)

Michael Jackson and Lenny Henry (29 August 1958)

Neil Harvey and Bill Maynard (8 October 1928)

George Foreman and Linda Lovelace (10 January 1949)

Goran Ivanisevic and Stella McCartney (13 September 1971)

Manfred Mann and Geoffrey Boycott (21 October 1940)

Meryl Streep and Lindsay Wagner (22 June 1949)

Marlon Brando and Doris Day (3 April 1924)

Stanley Kubrick and Danny La Rue (26 July 1928)

Billy the Kid and Halmar Branting, Prime Minister of Sweden (23 November 1860)

Yoko Ono and Bobby Robson (18 February 1933)

Harrison Ford and Roger McGuinn (13 July 1942)

Charles Dance and Chris Tarrant (10 October 1946)

Gene Wilder and Jackie Stewart (11 June 1939)

Prince Andrew and Leslie Ash (19 February 1960)

Hillary Rodham Clinton and Jaclyn Smith (26 October 1947)

Meat Loaf and Barbara Dickson (27 September 1947)

A Duck House
Ducks like water, but are very susceptible to damp, and it is therefore important to give them dry quarters.

TOP TEN CURRY HOUSE SONGS

'Poppadom Preach' – Madonna
'Korma Chameleon' – Culture Club
'Tikka Chance On Me' – Abba
'Argy Bhaji' – Squeeze
'It's My Chapati and I'll Cry If I Want To'
– Dave Stewart and Barbara Gaskin
'Tears On My Pilau' – Kylie Minogue
'Love Me Tandoor' – Elvis Presley
'Living Dhal' – Cliff Richard
'Paperback Raita' – Beatles
'Chicken Tikka . . . You and I Know' – Abba

SOME INTERESTING WAGERS

Three streakers to appear at the 2006 World Cup: 7–1

Life on Mars: 16–1

Britney Spears to catch husband Kevin Federline cheating on her
before the end of 2006: 18–1

Jack Charlton to become next Irish President: 100–1

Rosie Henman (Tim's three-year-old daughter) to win
Wimbledon one day: 250–1

Britney Spears to become US President: 500–1

Elvis to be still alive: 1,000–1

The Second Coming: 1,000–1

Discovery of the Loch Ness Monster: 2,000–1

Michael and LaToya Jackson proving to be the same person:
2,000–1

William Hill also took bets on what hairstyle David Beckham
would be sporting in England's opening game at the
2006 World Cup. The odds were:

Messy crop: Evens
Bald: 3–1
Alice band: 4–1
Spikey: 5–1
Ponytail: 8–1
Quiff: 8–1
Mullet: 10–1
That he'd have the name of one or all of his children spelled
out in his hair: 10–1
Pudding basin: 12–1
Dreadlocks: 33–1
Flat-top: 33–1
Wig: 100–1
Others: 200–1

USEFUL ARTILLERY PIECES

13-pounder field gun
105-mm field howitzer
35-mm triple-A cannon
25-pounder field gun
155-mm howitzer
6-pounder anti-tank gun
20-cm howitzer
88-mm PAK/FLAK (anti-tank/anti-aircraft)
2-pounder pom-pom
6-inch carriage-mounted naval gun

YOU'RE FIRED! CELEBRITY SACKINGS

Barbara Windsor was fired from her job as an assistant in a north London shoe shop because her highly effective bottom-wiggling sales routine upset the manageress.

George Michael was sacked from his Saturday job at British Home Stores for not wearing a shirt and tie in the stockroom.

Madonna was fired from her job as a waitress at fast-food restaurant Dunkin' Donuts for squirting jam at a customer.

Roger Moore was sacked as an office boy with a London cartoon firm for his inability to make a decent cup of tea.

Eric Sykes was fired from a cotton mill for singing 'The Blue of the Night' with a bucket on his head.

Robert Mitchum was fired from his job at an Ohio car factory over his refusal to wear socks.

Boy George was dismissed from his job as a Tesco's shelf-stacker for wearing the store's carrier bags. The company considered his appearance 'disturbing'.

Sidney Poitier was fired from his job parking cars because he couldn't drive. He confused first gear and reverse and ploughed into another car.

Alexei Sayle was sacked as assistant caretaker of a Fulham school for skiving off work early. He was grassed up by the school's lollipop man.

Dusty Springfield was sacked from her sales job at Bentalls after fusing the store's entire electrical system.

ROMAN EMPERORS AND THEIR PECCADILLOES

Caligula: Passed a law making it illegal for anyone to look at him in the street; used to smear prisoners with honey before setting loose an army of red wasps; invited his favourite horse, Incitatus, to dinner and wanted to make the animal a consul of the Roman Empire.

Nero: Ordered people to be executed for having a funny walk; had a young male slave, Sporus, castrated, dressed in women's clothes and renamed 'Sabina' to take the place of his late wife.

Tiberius: Forced victims to drink copious amounts of wine until their bladders were ready to burst, and then bound their genitals with a lute string.

Vitellius: A glutton who ate four huge meals a day and used to stick a feather down his throat between courses so that he vomited it all up and was therefore ready for the next course; had a pathological hatred of jugglers.

Domitian: His chosen form of torture was to hold a burning torch beneath prisoners' genitals.

Commodus: For entertainment, he liked to watch fights to the death between rival dwarfs with meat cleavers.

Elagabalus: Frequently posed as a female prostitute in the taverns of Rome; rounded up men with small penises and had them paraded naked through the streets to their execution; threw poisonous snakes at dinner guests; presided over a marriage between two rocks.

SOME ACTORS WHO HAVE
PLAYED DENTISTS IN MOVIES

Armand Assante
(*Consequence*): a dentist who
fakes his own death in an
insurance scam.

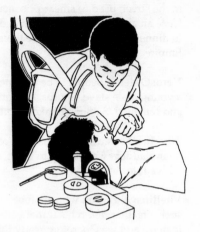

Corbin Bernsen (*The Dentist*
and *The Dentist 2*): a dentist
who turns sadist when he
realizes his wife is cheating on
him.

Norman Bird (*The Secret
Partner*): an alcoholic,
blackmailing dentist who is
forced to rob a businessman.

Daniel Day Lewis (*Eversmile, New Jersey*): a travelling dentist
spreading oral hygiene throughout South America.

Jochen Blume (*The Counterfeit Traitor*): an underground espionage
dentist in Hamburg.

Walter Matthau (*Cactus Flower*): a deceitful dentist who uses his
assistant to trick his girlfriend.

James Cagney (*The Strawberry Blonde*): an ex-con dentist involved
in a love triangle.

Laurence Olivier (*Marathon Man*): an evil Nazi dentist determined
to get his hands on a cache of diamonds.

Campbell Scott and **Hope Davis** (*The Secret Lives of Dentists*):
husband and wife dentists with a rocky marriage.

Julia Ormond (*Captives*): a prison dentist who foolishly gets
involved with one of her patients.

John Malkovich (*Rocket to the Moon*): a dentist with a failing practice and marriage who becomes involved with his attractive assistant.

Joel McCrea (*The Great Moment*): a pioneering dentist who tries to get laughing gas accepted as an anaesthetic.

GRANDSTAND PRESENTERS

Peter Dimmock
Frank Bough
Steve Rider
David Vine
Clare Balding
Bob Wilson
Helen Rollason
Ray Stubbs
Sue Barker

David Coleman
Desmond Lynam
Alan Weeks
Dougie Donnelly
Hazel Irvine
Harry Carpenter
Tony Gubba
John Inverdale

TEN AUTHORS TO CITE (EVEN IF YOU HAVEN'T READ THEM)

Alain Robbe-Grillet
F. R. Leavis
John Dos Passos
Louis-Ferdinand Céline (Louis-Ferdinand Destouches)
Stephen Hawking
'H. D.' (Hilda Doolittle)
Jack Kerouac
Arthur Rimbaud
Salman Rushdie
Gerard Manley Hopkins

INSIGHTFUL QUOTES ABOUT TREES

'You should go to a pear tree for pears, not to an elm.'
PUBILIUS SYRUS

'You will find something more in woods than in books.
Trees and stones will teach you that which you can never
learn from masters.'
ST BERNARD

'He that climbs the tall tree has won right to the fruit.'
SIR WALTER SCOTT

'It is difficult to realize how great a part of all that is cheerful
and delightful in the recollections of our own life is
associated with trees.'
WILSON FLAGG

'He that plants trees loves others beside himself.'
DR THOMAS FULLER

'Train up a fig tree in the way it should go, and when you are old
sit under the shade of it.'
CHARLES DICKENS

'Trees outstrip most people in the extent and depth of their work
for the public good.'
SARA EBENRECK

'The trees that are slow to grow bear the best fruit.'
MOLIÈRE

'Between every two pines is a doorway to a new world.'
JOHN MUIR

'There's nothing that keeps its youth,
So far as I know, but a tree and truth.'
OLIVER WENDELL HOLMES

How to lift a Rabbit.
The main part of the weight is carried by the hand under the rump. Some people prefer to lift by the scruff instead of the ears.

RANDOM ATOMIC NUMBERS OF CHEMICAL ELEMENTS

Erbium: 68   Berkelium: 97   Vanadium: 23   Indium: 49
Osmium: 76   Yttrium: 39   Tellurium: 52   Beryllium: 4

PRODUCTS AND OTHER STUFF THAT MIGHT HAVE TAKEN THEIR NAMES FROM FAMOUS PEOPLE

Potato crisps (Quentin Crisp)   Palindrome (Michael Palin)
Fruitellas (Ella Fitzgerald)   Almonds (Marc Almond)
M&Ms (Eminem)   Sunny D (Jack Dee)
Anagram (Anna Friel)   Mammogram (Mama Cass)
Telegram (Telly Savalas)   Flora (Dame Flora Robson)
KP Nuts (Kevin Pietersen)   Baskets (Alan Whicker)

CHRISTIAN NAMES AND THEIR MEANINGS

Adrian – the dark one
Alison – of sacred fame
Anthea – flower-like
Arnold – strong as an eagle
Barry – javelin
Benjamin – son of the right hand
Beverley – from a beaver meadow
Dale – frequenter of gatherings
Doris – of the sea
Edward – property guardian
Emma – all embracing
Geraldine – mighty with a spear
Jasper – bearer of treasure
Jemima – dove
Jessica – woman of wealth
Leigh – weary
Linda – serpent
Louise – famous in battle
Madeline – tower
Mavis – thrush
Melissa – honey bee
Miriam – rebellious
Norma – model
Pamela – sweet as honey
Paul – small
Percy – gorge-piercer
Philip – horse lover
Simon – visionary
Tess – harvester
Tony – beyond praise
Vanessa – butterfly
Wayne – wagon-maker
Wendy – wanderer
Yvonne – young archer

SOME LANDMARKS THAT FEATURE ON THE WIGAN VERSION OF MONOPOLY

Uncle Joe's Mint Balls Factory
Spinning Gate Shopping Centre, Leigh
Coliseum, Hilton Park, home of Leigh Rugby Football Club
Three Sisters Recreation Area
Turnpike Centre, which houses Leigh Library
Wigan International Jazz Festival
Pennington Flash Country Park
Patak's Indian Food Factory
Wigan Warriors rugby league team
The Galleries Shopping Centre
Haigh Hall
JJB Stadium

THINGS THAT PROVE A TURN-OFF FOR HOUSE BUYERS

A week's washing-up in the sink
A corpse in the lounge
A bedroom that is a shrine to *Star Trek*
Moss growing on the damp walls
Metal grilles on the windows
Neighbours called Mengele
A 'Beware of Subsidence' sign in the front garden
A resident ghost
Blood on the walls
A suffocating smell of gas
Ann Maurice

SOME GUEST ARTISTS ON *THE SIMPSONS*

Tony Bennett as himself
Ringo Starr as himself
Dustin Hoffman as Mr Bergstrom
Kelsey Grammer as Sideshow Bob
Michael Jackson as Leon Kompowsky
Aerosmith as themselves
Sting as himself
Joe Frazier as himself
Bob Hope as himself
Tom Jones as himself
Leonard Nimoy as himself
Elizabeth Taylor as the voice of Maggie
Brooke Shields as herself
Barry White as himself
The Red Hot Chili Peppers as themselves
George Harrison as himself
Michelle Pfeiffer as Mindy Simmons
Meryl Streep as Jessica Lovejoy
Mel Brooks as himself
Paul and Linda McCartney as themselves
Kirk Douglas as Chester J. Lampwick
Johnny Cash as the Coyote
U2 as themselves
Steve Martin as Ray Patterson
Jerry Springer as himself
Kim Basinger as herself
The Moody Blues as themselves
Cyndi Lauper as herself
Elton John as himself
Stephen Hawking as himself
Mel Gibson as himself
Britney Spears as herself
The Who as themselves
Andre Agassi as himself
Pete Sampras as himself
Serena and Venus Williams as themselves
R.E.M. as themselves
Paul Newman as himself

Richard Gere as himself
Mick Jagger as himself
Little Richard as himself
David Byrne as himself
Tony Blair as himself
Ian McKellen as himself
J.K. Rowling as herself
Simon Cowell as Henry
Sarah Michelle Gellar as Gina Vendetti
50 Cent as himself
Dennis Rodman as himself
Ricky Gervais as Charles
Larry Hagman as Wallace Brady

BIG (WELL, BIGGISH) BRITISH MAMMALS

Grey seal	Red deer
Walrus (an occasional visitor)	Porpoise
Right whale	Badger
Fallow deer	Wildcat
Red fox	Atlantic seal

Dosing a Dog (single-handed).
Dog's nose held with one hand while the
other presses neck of phial into angle of lips.

Dosing a Dog
(two persons).

THE FUTURE'S RIGHT WITH OLD SHITE

YOUR HOROSCOPE FOR 2007

ARIES (21 MARCH–20 APRIL)
Birthstone: Diamond
Lucky Vegetable: Radish
Lucky Celebrity: Tamzin Outhwaite

January: This is a hectic month, but beware of someone who may hold a grudge against you. There will be an opportunity to put your people skills to the test when the police raid your house and seize your hard drive on the 27th.

February: Unexpected news could make you reassess your plans for the future. A chance meeting may lead to a lasting friendship. Money matters come to the fore around the middle of the month. At some point between the 16th and the 23rd you will get wet.

March: Someone close to you will ask for your advice, but you may need to refrain from saying what you really think. You will receive either an exciting new job offer or your P45. Watch out for falling masonry.

April: The influence of Venus makes this a significant period for affairs of the heart and you should not be shy about taking the lead in such matters. Definitely a time for grabbing the bull by the horns and milking it!

May: Opportunities for travel arise in the first week of the month, but these may have to be put on hold. Your social expertise makes you popular with colleagues except the bitch in Sales and Marketing. A frozen cod steak causes concern.

June: The grass is always greener on the other side of the fence. There's many a slip 'twixt cup and lip. Too many cooks spoil the broth. A stitch in time saves nine. The darkest hour is just before dawn.

July: A surprise announcement around the 10th causes you to take stock of your wardrobe. A slow-moving stranger in an orange and navy-blue jacket brings news. You are asked to take part in a group activity, but you should check for two-way mirrors and *News of the World* investigative reporters.

August: Be flexible over relationships and look after your health. Now could be a good time for planning an ascent of the north face of the Eiger. Someone you know has a headache.

September: Nothing happening for you this month.

October: A close relative is abducted by aliens. Your chewing gum loses its flavour on the bedpost overnight. A chance meeting with Dale Winton ends in heartbreak. You may encounter some weather.

November: Don't keep your feelings to yourself. Try A1 Counselling, 49 Hanging Gardens of Babylon View, Basingstoke (Mon–Fri 9–5, £35 per session; £70 for schizophrenics).

December: Christmas happens: deal with it.

TAURUS (21 APRIL–21 MAY)
Birthstone: Emerald
Lucky Vegetable: Turnip
Lucky Celebrity: Pliny the Elder

January: Financial matters may be on your mind in the third week, but the security van robbery you are planning is no solution. Eat plenty of cheese.

February: Don't let others exploit you. Don't overtake approaching a pedestrian crossing. Don't use mobile phones in the library. Keep off the grass.

March: Your partner gives you the opportunity to travel by dumping your bags on the doorstep. A change of scenery could be just what you need. A crazed elk throws your world into turmoil.

April: A passionate encounter in the Diana Memorial Fountain leads to an unexpected meeting with a police officer and the duty solicitor. Avoid Tuesdays like the plague.

May: Pull yourself together, for God's sake! You're a pathetic excuse for a human being. Flogging's too good for you. National Service is what you need!

June: The influence of Pluto causes you to start burying bones in the garden.

July: An offer leaves you in a dilemma. Every day brings fresh news. Your fingernails grow. An acquaintance speaks to you.

August: Changes are afoot in your life and you could seize the chance of turning a problem to your advantage. Don't let a madman wielding an axe deter you from your chosen path. Lucky fish: the stickleback.

September: If you go down to the woods today, you're sure of a big surprise.

October: You have a dream in which you are the feared Viking warrior Harald Hardrada, but you should nevertheless resist the temptation to pillage and raze vast swathes of North Yorkshire. It will only end in upset.

November: The opportunity arises to spice up your sex life, but you need to break free from domestic ties in case the neighbours are watching.

December: Some decisions you make are good, some are bad. Others are somewhere in-between. A persistent itch could prove troublesome.

GEMINI (22 MAY–21 JUNE)
Birthstone: Agate
Lucky Vegetable: Courgette
Lucky Celebrity: Joe 'Mr Piano' Henderson

January: You are the life and soul of the gathering, cracking jokes, singing bawdy songs and leading everyone in the conga. Not all of the mourners approve, however.

February: You should keep risks to a minimum. Therefore stay indoors – you never know what's out there.

March: Career prospects abound. There is a chance to step up the ladder – maybe even hold the bucket. Friends rally round in a time of need. An unexpected windfall soils your pants.

April: Sawing your own leg off may seem a good idea, but is it really worth it just to get rid of that tiny blemish? Seek a friend's advice before embarking on such drastic action. Lucky Royal: Queen Juliana of the Netherlands.

May: A friend is in desperate need of a favour, but sometimes the best helping hand you can give is a good, firm push. From the 21st onwards, you will be preparing for a birthday.

June: If everything's going your way, it probably means you're driving in the wrong lane. An unsettling experience with a garden gnome leads you to reassess your priorities.

July: A good month for a holiday. Close relatives are unsympathetic when you try to poison them. A marauding badger spoils a dinner party.

August: The influence of Mars causes you to put on weight and come out in acne. Don't trim your toenails at the dinner table.

September: Think twice before sending a strippergram to the harvest festival.

October: Your partner is disturbed to find you in bed with a workmate. Everybody else keeps theirs in the shed.

November: This could be the time to take a gamble with money – you may be lucky. Or you may end up losing your house, car and family. And remember: two heads are better than one – unless it's actually a deformity.

December: Decisions have to be made. Night follows day. A man in a red coat and with a bushy white beard comes into your life. Lucky Marx Brother: Chico.

CANCER (22 JUNE–22 JULY)
Birthstone: Ruby
Lucky Vegetable: Shallot
Lucky Celebrity: Hereward the Wake

January: Life's what you make it. There are more questions than answers. The only way is up. Smile like you mean it. Don't let the sun catch you crying. Blame it on the pony express. There's a guy works down the chipshop swears he's Elvis.

February: A friend comes up with an interesting proposition involving a goat, some ice cream and a pair of rubber gloves. A close relative comes back from the dead.

March: If at first you don't succeed, then skydiving probably isn't for you.

April: You work hard to restore the status quo. Rick Parfitt's face in particular requires a lot of attention. Money could be tight towards the middle of the month or you could win the lottery. Lucky newsreader: Matthew Amroliwala

May: A favourable second phase of the moon in Jupiter's orbit makes this the ideal month for stewing prunes.

June: See September.

July: Look after your health. Try not to let anyone mug you. Don't step in front of a bus as it's about to pull away. There could be problems with a reluctant deckchair.

August: Be afraid, be very afraid.

September: See June.

October: When the chips are down, pick them off the floor and get on with cooking dinner. Workmen drilling outside your house will give you a headache.

November: A friend in desperate need confides in you and wants you to be a permanent shoulder to cry on. Tell them to get a life. Lucky kitchen utensil: the egg whisk.

December: A good month for giving presents.

LEO (23 JULY–23 AUGUST)
Birthstone: Sapphire
Lucky Vegetable: Swede
Lucky Celebrity: Tara Palmer-Tomkinson

January: Everywhere you look there are weasels: weasels in cupboards, weasels under the bed, weasels in the wardrobe. Go to your doctor and suggest a change in medication.

February: Life seems to be dealing you a rough hand, particularly around the third week of the month. Try to be philosophical about it. Accept that some days you're the pigeon and some days you're the statue.

March: Good news: a chance meeting with a stranger presents you with an opportunity to travel. Bad news: he's kidnapping you.

April: You should be cautious in financial matters. A proposition that may appear too good to refuse could have hidden dangers. Don't wear blue and brown – they just don't go together.

May: A good time for new contacts – you're struggling to see out of the old ones. Be wary of anyone carrying a machine gun. Lucky US President: Warren G. Harding.

June: A tight conjunction around Uranus means there is plenty of scope for cheap jokes.

July: Friends and colleagues can be unreliable and you should treat flattery with caution because, let's face it, you're bloody ugly. If you think nobody cares about you, try missing a couple of mortgage payments.

August: You may be the recipient of some extraordinarily good news. Then again . . .

September: Remember your chip and PIN number.

October: The full moon on the 26th falls in Leo in the tenth house. To avoid damage that night, move to number twelve.

November: A sudden tax demand throws your finances into chaos, the bailiffs repossess your furniture, and your partner runs off with your best friend. Lucky day: Wednesday.

December: A time for exciting social encounters. Don't overextend yourself when reaching for that jar of mayonnaise on the top shelf. Don't sleep in the subway, darling, don't stand in the pouring rain.

VIRGO (24 AUGUST–23 SEPTEMBER)
Birthstone: Sardonyx
Lucky Vegetable: Cauliflower
Lucky Celebrity: Hermann Goering

January: A chance to realize your ambitions as your career plans fall into place. Don't be afraid to aim higher than usual – unless it means splashing the wall.

February: After the joy of January, it's back down to earth with an unsettling period around the middle of the month. Relationship and health matters cause concern, and you ponder the wisdom of accepting a new job. It's a long way to travel and the salary is nothing exceptional. But the biggest drawback is an elephant's foreskin.

March: Despair sets in as a loved one sends you reeling with a left hook and some devastating news. Close family will prove a real burden at this time. You also have trouble programming the video.

April: Don't throw your weight around at home – it could cause structural damage.

May: This month sees harmonious relationships between Mercury, Venus, Jupiter and Saturn. It's so nice to see them getting along.

June: Throw all your energy into pleasurable pursuits, but don't forget to draw the curtains first. Oxygen is in the air.

July: You are in great demand, but a false moustache and a fake passport preserve your liberty. And remember: change is inevitable, except from a vending machine. Lucky cloud: Nimbostratus.

August: A lucky phase when you should make the most of material possessions. Dandruff is a problem around the 19th. Watch out, watch out, there's a Humphrey about.

September: Your willingness to help others reaps its reward. You go out with an agoraphobic, well perhaps not *out* . . .

October: Keep your eyes open, especially when crossing the road. It's much safer that way.

November: The full moon on the 24th falls in Virgo in the seventh house, thereby highlighting issues relating to dental flossing. Give those teeth an extra brush.

December: Key decisions leave you in a quandary. Is it the one for the front door or the back door? Avoid confrontations, especially with armed police officers.

LIBRA (24 SEPTEMBER–23 OCTOBER)
Birthstone: Opal
Lucky Vegetable: Lentil
Lucky Celebrities: Keith Harris and Orville

January: You thrive on extra responsibility at work, as others come to appreciate your qualities. If you can smile when things go wrong, you've probably thought of someone to blame.

February: A time to make important relationship decisions. Do you really want to spend the rest of your life with someone who has the national collection of Sonia CDs?

March: Influences this month suggest this is a good time to invest in a new pair of socks. Beware of Greeks baring bottoms. Lucky number: 1,246,359.

April: A small flutter on the Grand National could prove profitable. Choose a horse that still has a jockey on board at the end of the race. A juggler turns your world upside down.

May: Affairs of the heart bring out the best rather than the beast in you. A course in martial arts will encourage others to come round to your way of thinking. Something comes unexpectedly to the surface – it's a floater.

June: Laughter is the best medicine – unless you're really sick, in which case you should call 999. Resist the temptation to take up stamp collecting – philately will get you nowhere.

July: A friend tries to put you on the spot, little realizing that Clearasil is more effective. A horse's head in your bed may prove upsetting.

August: The new moon on the 12th falls in Libra in conjunction with Mercury. This points to a huge upheaval in world markets, possibly resulting in the collapse of several major financial institutions and an unprecedented panic on the pound. So don't forget to pay that library fine. Lucky human body part: the pancreas.

September: Life is full of little irritations, but the school holidays are almost over. Avoid clichés like the plague. Speak clearly after the tone.

October: Life is a minestrone, served up with parmesan cheese. Death is a cold lasagne, suspended in deep freeze.

November: Now could be a good time to boost your social life. Perhaps you should do something about your hair, smarten yourself up a bit and pay closer attention to personal hygiene. Fungal foot infections aren't cool, you know. And those smelly old trainers should have been thrown out years ago. An encounter with HM Revenue & Customs proves taxing. You may start hearing voices in your head.

December: An infestation of coypu threatens your very existence. A face from the past gives you a surprise – you thought you'd buried him under the patio ten years ago.

SCORPIO (24 OCTOBER–22 NOVEMBER)
Birthstone: Topaz
Lucky Vegetable: Parsnip
Lucky Celebrity: Judith Chalmers

January: A good month for making an impression, but don't do Elvis – everybody does him. Towards the end of the month an experience with pasta spirals proves traumatic.

February: Conflicts at work leave you disheartened. But resist the urge to fight fire with fire, because water is usually much more effective.

March: A period of minor hiccups: try holding your breath for a minute. Crossing the Severn Bridge takes its toll.

April: Pace yourself and don't waste energy, particularly with gas prices being so high. And don't forget, honesty is always the best policy, although insanity is a better defence. Lucky London Underground station: Tooting Broadway.

May: Avoid getting into conversations with Russians, unless there is a translator present.

June: A time for renewed optimism when everything seems to be going your way. Take a chance on a new relationship – it could lead to lasting happiness – and revel in the opportunity to explore fresh horizons. A dream job offer convinces you that things are definitely on the up. The world may end on the 19th.

July: Don't leave home without it.

August: Planetary influences indicate that the 24th is a perfect day for getting out and about with your dog. But don't take him dancing – he's got two left feet.

September: When an escaped wife terrorizes the neighbourhood, you see an opportunity to make capital out of the chaos. But remember: those who live by the sword get shot by those who don't.

October: Be wary of making rash purchases, although it could be an opportune moment to invest in a new umbrella. Between the 19th and the 21st there will be a Saturday. Lucky insect order: Orthoptera.

November: A facelift proves expensive. Watch out for the bogey man.

December: The ascendancy of Neptune in the third quarter suggests this is a good time for de-lousing the hair of a loved one.

SAGITTARIUS (23 NOVEMBER–21 DECEMBER)
Birthstone: Turquoise
Lucky Vegetable: Broad bean
Lucky Celebrity: Ethelred the Unready

January: An interesting time for exchanging new ideas and unwanted Christmas presents. Exercise zero tolerance in all relationship matters because an iron fist in an iron glove will prove beneficial in the long run – unless you're a surgeon.

February: The alignment of Mercury and Saturn points to the fact that someone you know will suffer from a cold or some other ailment this month. At work, pride comes before a fall, as do six lagers and a tricky flight of steps.

March: Life goes on.

April: A good time for boring the pants off people. There may be a worrying incident when you fall into an upholstery machine. Happily, you will soon be fully recovered.

May: Career developments are strongly highlighted, but don't be tempted to overreach your capabilities. A bird in the hand is safer than one overhead.

June: Don't make hasty decisions. Don't let others take advantage of your good nature. Don't streak down the High Street when there's a police patrol car outside Woolworths.

July: July has been cancelled for Sagittarians.

August: Relationship matters may or may not cause problems. If you don't want to feel left out in the cold, remember to take your door key. Lucky *Trumpton* Character: Barney McGrew.

September: A time for helping others less fortunate than yourself. Do not stint on charitable deeds, particularly if they involve overseas travel. You may think about becoming a missionary – it's always a popular position.

October: Armed penguins hold your family hostage. Do not be swayed by their fine plumage.

November: The location of the planets indicates that this is a time to be assertive and single-minded in your career, providing it's all right with everyone else.

December: Beware of meeting a fat man in a red suit in a confined space – Santaclaustrophobia is becoming alarmingly common.

CAPRICORN (22 DECEMBER–20 JANUARY)
Birthstone: Garnet
Lucky Vegetable: Sweetcorn
Lucky Celebrities: Elsie and Doris Waters

January: An important time for making new friends and business contacts as your communication skills reap rewards. People who had previously taken you for granted now start to see you in a new light. On the 3rd you turn into a werewolf.

February: As well as meeting people from different walks of life, try meeting people with different walks – the high-stepper, the tiptoe-trotter, the shambling shuffler. The 29th won't happen.

March: Think carefully before adding to your material possessions. Do you really need yet another pair of shoes? What's wrong with the pair you bought last month? The actions of a rogue hamster may necessitate surgery.

April: Venus in your sign suggests the start of a new love interest. Don't be put off by first appearances. A glass eye can be very attractive.

May: A tricky sort of month when calamity could be just around the corner for those who fail to exercise caution. So don't take financial risks, don't push your luck in relationships and, most important of all, don't walk on the cracks in the pavement.

June: People respond positively to your natural generosity. Remember: one good turn gets most of the blankets.

July: The major focus this month is on petunias.

August: Be careful about making mistakes – they're not a good idea. You may feel the need to slow down approaching a speed camera. An electrical appliance holds you hostage. Lucky antelope: Jentink's duiker.

September: Opt for a stable life, even though the straw irritates your eczema. Avoid Jehovah's Witnesses – you'll never get rid of them. Plan to have your hair cut around the 11th.

October: You receive a nasty shock when you are told that your Afghan hound has been arrested for dogging. You may also be the subject of unsubstantiated rumours regarding a nun, a Dyson upright and a knob of butter.

November: Although monetary matters are positively highlighted, resist the temptation to gamble your life savings on Linda's Delight in the 2.30 at Catterick. It will finish only fourth. And never argue with a spouse who is packing your parachute.

December: Instead of living life in the fast lane, enjoy a spell in the bus lane. Look out for a full moon at the office party.

AQUARIUS (21 JANUARY–19 FEBRUARY)
Birthstone: Amethyst
Lucky Vegetable: Mushy Peas
Lucky Celebrity: Plastic Bertrand

January: The first week of the month appears propitious for unicycling. With Mars in your opposite house of attraction, look to starting a war with a small nation.

February: Romantic thoughts may be in the air around the 14th. There could be stress in concrete.

March: Participation in an international gargling competition may end in disappointment. Your fortunes are favoured around the third week, but never underestimate the power of stupid people in large groups. Towards the end of the month the ten of diamonds could be on the cards.

April: Financial and relationship matters receive negative planetary highlights: Neptune and Saturn seem to be ganging up on you. But in what could prove a difficult time, keep your chin up – even if it requires surgery.

May: A time for planning the future and considering various job options. Don't put all your eggs in one basket, especially if you're in the 'Five items or fewer' queue at the supermarket.

June: A word in the right ear might improve your chances of getting a pay rise; a word in the left ear will be pointless – your boss is deaf in that one. And always be sincere, even if you don't mean it.

July: The 9th is a lucky day for having boils lanced.

August: Life goes smoothly, apart from the odd bumpy bits. As the sun moves into your sign, don't forget the factor 15.

September: There could be an opportunity to travel – don't forget to pack your toothbrush. A hotel lift is in the ascendant around the 16th. Lucky screw: the three-eighths pan head Phillips.

October: Take time for a period of reflection in the bathroom mirror. Personal relationships and rattlesnakes should be handled with care.

November: If everyone about you is losing their head while you are keeping yours, it could be that you haven't understood the problem. There may be fireworks around the 5th.

December: Think carefully before making important decisions. Don't go for a clifftop stroll with a lemming. Never hit a man with glasses – hit him with something bigger and heavier.

PISCES (20 FEBRUARY–20 MARCH)
Birthstone: Bloodstone
Lucky Vegetable: Beetroot
Lucky Celebrity: Abraham Darby

January: Re-stringing a tennis racket could cause tension. You may find yourself being arrested as a KGB spy around the 11th and facing torture and deportation, but try to look on the bright side. Be prepared for a let-down with an inflatable partner.

February: Unexpected events may take you by surprise.

March: Avoid major undertakings, at least until you've bought a hearse. A good month for washing your hair. Lucky road: B1223 (Selby to Towton).

April: With Neptune at its shyest and hiding behind the sofa, the omens suggest that any fillet steaks cooked that day should be done medium rare. Lending a large sum of money to a complete stranger could prove risky.

May: The first week is the best part of the month for you. Be sympathetic to friends and you will see tangible rewards. You may also receive good news concerning a health matter that has been troubling you. Around the 20th a skateboarding duck blights your happiness.

June: Try not to take the worries of the world on your shoulders but if you are run down, don't forget to take the licence number. Growing your own strawberries may prove fruitful.

July: It's a time for making your dreams come true – except the one where you're chased naked by a 20-foot-high Graham Norton through a field of stinging nettles.

August: Consider the benefits of cavity wall insulation. Be alert: the world needs more lerts.

September: Don't let your goldfish bully you into buying it a new bowl – you need to impose your authority once and for all. Cardiac surgery may leave you disheartened.

October: Eat a bowl of cold vomit first thing in the morning. That way, nothing worse can happen to you for the rest of the day.

November: An untrained Labrador could turn your room upside down. Think twice before lending your passport to someone who has just escaped from prison. Lucky algebraic calculation: the simultaneous equation.

December: You should start seeing things more clearly if you invest in a pair of binoculars. But a period of gloom descends around the 6th – you may have forgotten to pay your electricity bill.

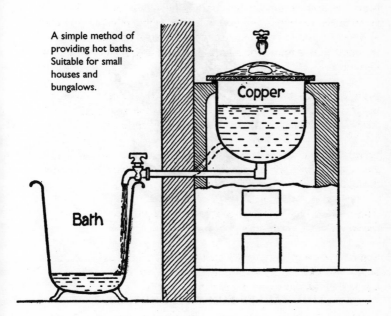

A simple method of providing hot baths. Suitable for small houses and bungalows.

LIGHTING-UP TIMES FOR 1 JANUARY 2007

Cigarettes: 5.04 p.m.   Cigars: 5.12 p.m.   Pipes: 5.33 p.m.

TIDE TABLES FOR WATFORD*, 2007

1 January, high water: 2.32, 14.55
2 January, high water: 3.14, 15.38
3 January, high water: 3.50, 16.19
You can work the rest out yourself.

* Add 21 min for Hemel Hempstead, 1 hr 03 min for High Wycombe, subtract 48 min for Pinner.

YOUR DAY-BY-DAY GUIDE TO 2007

JANUARY

1 Mon: Sigismund I of Poland, b. 1467; Maurice Chevalier, d. 1972; Independence Day, Cameroon.

2 Tues: Roger Miller, b. 1936; Ovid, d. AD 17; Berchtold's Day, Switzerland.

3 Wed: Michael Schumacher, b. 1969; William Joyce ('Lord Haw-Haw'), d. 1946; Revolution Day, Burkina Faso.

4 Thurs: Michael Stipe, b. 1960; Albert Camus, d. 1960; Martyrs' Day, Zaire.

5 Fri: Diane Keaton, b. 1946; Edward the Confessor, d. 1066.

6 Sat: Rowan Atkinson, b. 1955; Theodore Roosevelt, d. 1919; Children's Day, Uruguay.

7 Sun: Helen Worth, b. 1951; Catherine of Aragon, d. 1536; Trevor Howard, d. 1988.

8 Mon: David Bowie, b. 1947; Galileo, d. 1642; Midwife's Day, Greece.

9 Tues: Richard Nixon, b. 1913; Jimmy Page, b. 1944; Napoleon III, d. 1873.

10 Wed: Rod Stewart, b. 1945; George Foreman, b. 1949; Coco Chanel, d. 1971.

11 Thurs: Arthur Scargill, b. 1938; Thomas Hardy, d. 1928; Hostos Day, Puerto Rico.

12 Fri: Mel C, b. 1974; Isaac Pitman, d. 1897; Revolution Day, Tanzania.

13 Sat: Stephen Hendry, b. 1969; James Joyce, d. 1941; Liberation Day, Togo.

14 Sun: Faye Dunaway, b. 1941; Humphrey Bogart, d. 1957; Thaipoosam Cavadee, Mauritius.

15 Mon: Pete Waterman, b. 1947; Emma, Lady Hamilton, d. 1815; Teacher's Day, Venezuela; Adult's Day, Japan.

16 Tues: Ethel Merman, b. 1909; Kate Moss, b. 1974; Edmund Spenser, d. 1599.

17 Wed: Muhammad Ali, b. 1942; Jim Carrey, b. 1962; Francis Galton, d. 1911.

18 Thurs: David Bellamy, b. 1933; Kevin Costner, b. 1955; Cecil Beaton, d. 1980.

19 Fri: Dolly Parton, b. 1946; Jenson Button, b. 1980; William Congreve, d. 1729.

20 Sat: Federico Fellini, b. 1920; Charles VII of Bavaria, d. 1745; National Holiday, Armenia.

21 Sun: Jack Nicklaus, b. 1940; George Orwell, d. 1950; Altagracia Day, Dominican Republic.

22 Mon: Michael Hutchence, b. 1960; Queen Victoria, d. 1901; Discovery Day, St. Vincent.

23 Tues: Bob Paisley, b. 1919; Princess Caroline of Monaco, b. 1957; William Pitt the Younger, d. 1806.

24 Wed: Hadrian, b. AD 76; Neil Diamond, b. 1941; Winston Churchill, d. 1965.

25 Thurs: Virginia Woolf, b. 1882; Ava Gardner, d. 1990; Tatiana Day, Russia.

26 Fri: Paul Newman, b. 1925; General Gordon of Khartoum, d. 1885; Duarte Day, Dominican Republic.

27 Sat: Mark Owen, b. 1972; Giuseppe Verdi, d. 1901; St. Devota's Day, Monaco.

28 Sun: Henry VII, b. 1457; Frank Skinner, b. 1957; Francis Drake, d. 1596.

29 Mon: Frederick Delius, b. 1862; Oprah Winfrey, b. 1954; Alan Ladd, d. 1964.

30 Tues: Percy Thrower, b. 1913; Gene Hackman, b. 1930; Queen Alexandra of Yugoslavia, d. 1993.

31 Wed: Justin Timberlake, b. 1981; Winifred Atwell, d. 1983; Independence Day, Nauru.

Weather forecast for January: Some areas of Britain may see rain of varying amounts while others may remain dry from time to time. There will be some sunshine in certain places, particularly where the clouds break, as well as a risk of thunder and maybe fog. Where trees start blowing about, it will be windy. Snow, sleet and hail are also possible, but may not happen at all. Temperatures will be around, above or below normal. It will generally be dark at night, but lighter by day.

•

FEBRUARY

1 Thurs: Clark Gable, b. 1901; Peter Sallis, b. 1921; Buster Keaton, d. 1966.

2 Fri: Farrah Fawcett, b. 1947; Pope Clement XIII, d. 1769; Groundhog Day, USA.

3 Sat: Frankie Vaughan, b. 1928; Val Doonican, b. 1929; John of Gaunt, d. 1399.

4 Sun: Natalie Imbruglia, b. 1975; Liberace, d. 1987; Independence Day, Sri Lanka.

5 Mon: Russell Grant, b. 1952; Thomas Carlyle, d. 1881; Constitution Day, Mexico.

6 Tues: Axl Rose, b. 1962; Charles II, d. 1685; Waitangi Day, New Zealand.

7 Wed: Eddie Izzard, b. 1962; Gustavus IV of Sweden, d. 1837; Independence Day, Grenada.

8 Thurs: Jules Verne, b. 1828; Mary, Queen of Scots, d. 1587; Preseren Day, Slovenia

9 Fri: Gordon Strachan, b. 1957; Princess Margaret, d. 2002; St. Marion's Day, Lebanon.

10 Sat: Jimmy Durante, b. 1893; Sophie Tucker, d. 1966; St. Paul's Day, Malta.

11 Sun: Jennifer Aniston, b. 1969; Sylvia Plath, d. 1963; National Day, Iran.

12 Mon: Charles Darwin, b. 1809; Prince Naseem Hamed, b. 1974; Lillie Langtry, d. 1929.

13 Tues: Georges Simenon, b. 1901; Robbie Williams, b. 1974; Richard Wagner, d. 1883.

14 Wed: Kevin Keegan, b. 1951; Richard II, d. 1400, Captain James Cook, d. 1779; Fastelavn, Denmark.

15 Thurs: Matt Groening, b. 1954; Nat King Cole, d. 1965; John Frum Day, Vanuatu.

16 Fri: John McEnroe, b. 1959; Alfonso III of Portugal, d. 1279; Independence Day, Lithuania.

17 Sat: Barry Humphries, b. 1934; Tamurlane the Great, d. 1405; Geronimo, d. 1908.

18 Sun: John Travolta, b. 1954; Martin Luther, d. 1546; Independence Day, Gambia.

19 Mon: Copernicus, b. 1473; Ray Winstone, b. 1957; Charles Blondin, d. 1897.

20 Tues: Gordon Brown, b. 1951; Cindy Crawford, b. 1966; James I of Scotland, d. 1437.

21 Wed: Charlotte Church, b. 1986; Jethro Tull, d. 1741; Shaheed Day, Bangladesh.

22 Thurs: Steve Irwin, b. 1962; Drew Barrymore, b. 1975; Amerigo Vespucci, d. 1512.

23 Fri: Melinda Messenger, b. 1971; L.S. Lowry, d. 1976; National Day, Brunei.

24 Sat: Lleyton Hewitt, b. 1981; Henry Cavendish, d. 1810; National Day, Estonia.

25 Sun: David Puttnam, b.1941; Nick Leeson, b. 1967; Christopher Wren, d. 1723; People Power Day, Philippines.

26 Mon: Victor Hugo, b. 1802; Michael Bolton, b. 1953; Roger II of Sicily, d. 1154; Liberation Day, Kuwait.

27 Tues: Elizabeth Taylor, b. 1932; Alexander Porfirevich Borodin, d. 1887; Independence Day, Dominican Republic.

28 Wed: Thomas Newcomen, b. 1663; Brian Jones, b. 1942; Henry James, d. 1916.

Weather forecast for February: Some areas of Britain may see rain of varying amounts while others may remain dry from time to time. There will be some sunshine in certain places, particularly where the clouds break, as well as a risk of thunder and maybe fog. Where trees start blowing about, it will be windy. Snow, sleet and hail are also possible but may not happen at all. Temperatures will be around, above or below normal. It will generally be dark at night, but lighter by day.

•

MARCH

1 Thurs: Mike Read, b. 1951; Thomas Ellwood, d. 1713; Nuclear Bomb Victims' Day, Marshall Islands.

2 Fri: Jon Bon Jovi, b. 1962; D.H. Lawrence, d. 1930; Victory of Aduwa Day, Ethiopia; Peasants' Day, Myanmar.

3 Sat: Peter O'Sullevan, b. 1918; Danny Kaye, d. 1987; Makha Bucha Day, Thailand.

4 Sun: Shakin' Stevens, b. 1948; Kenny Dalglish, b. 1951; Saladin, d. 1193; Admission Day, Vermont.

5 Mon: Louis I of Hungary, b. 1326; Joseph Stalin, d. 1953; Discovery Day, Guam.

6 Tues: Cyrano de Bergerac, b. 1619; Davy Crockett, d. 1836; Green Monday, Greece; Custom Chiefs' Day, Vanuatu.

7 Wed: Henry Moore, b. 1831; Rik Mayall, b. 1958; Pope Innocent XIII, d. 1724; Teacher's Day, Albania.

8 Thurs: Mickey Dolenz, b. 1945; Gyles Brandreth, b. 1948; Louis-Hector Berlioz, d. 1869.

9 Fri: André Courreges, b. 1923; Yuri Gagarin, b. 1934; Cardinal Mazarin, d. 1661; Baron Bliss Day, Belize.

10 Sat: Sharon Stone, b. 1958; Ray Milland, d. 1986; Youth Day, Zambia.

11 Sun: Rupert Murdoch, b. 1931; Douglas Adams, b. 1952; Alexander Fleming, d. 1955; Johnny Appleseed Day, USA.

12 Mon: David Mellor, b. 1949; Arnold Ridley, d. 1984; Moshoeshoe's Day, Lesotho.

13 Tues: Neil Sedaka, b. 1939; Joe Bugner, b. 1950; Clarence Darrow, d. 1938.

14 Wed: Albert Einstein, b. 1879; Michael Caine, b. 1933; Karl Marx, d. 1883; White Day, Japan.

15 Thurs: Terence Trent D'Arby, b. 1962; Julius Caesar, d. 44 BC; Thora Hird, d. 2003; Constitution Day, Belarus.

16 Fri: Leo McKern, b. 1920; Jerry Lewis, b. 1926; Nero, d. AD 68.

17 Sat: Rudolf Nureyev, b. 1938; Kurt Russell, b. 1951; Harold Harefoot, King of England, d. 1040; Evacuation Day, Boston, Massachusetts.

18 Sun: Neville Chamberlain, b. 1869; Alex Higgins, b. 1949; Ivan the Terrible, d. 1584; Flag Day, Aruba.

19 Mon: Bruce Willis, b. 1955; Edgar Rice Burroughs, d. 1950; St Joseph's Day, Liechtenstein.

20 Tues: Henrik Ibsen, b. 1828; Vera Lynn, b. 1917; Isaac Newton, d. 1727.

21 Wed: Johann Sebastian Bach, b. 1685; Harry H. Corbett, d. 1982; Juarez Day, Mexico.

22 Thurs: William Shatner, b. 1931; Jean-Baptiste Lully, d. 1687; Abolition Day, Puerto Rico.

23 Fri: Margaret of Anjou, b. 1430; Joan Crawford, b. 1904; Pedro the Cruel, King of Castile, d. 1369; Republic Day, Pakistan.

24 Sat: Alan Sugar, b. 1947; Tommy Hilfiger, b. 1951; Queen Elizabeth I, d. 1603.

25 Sun: Elton John, b. 1947; Claude Debussy, d. 1918; Independence Day, Greece.

26 Mon: Diana Ross, b. 1944; Ludwig van Beethoven, d. 1827; Independence Day, Bangladesh.

27 Tues: Mariah Carey, b. 1970; Arnold Bennett, d. 1931; Evacuation Day, Angola.

28 Wed: Dirk Bogarde, b. 1921; Michael Parkinson, b. 1935; Dwight Eisenhower, d. 1969; Teacher's Day, Slovakia.

29 Thurs: Elle Macpherson, b. 1968; The Singing Nun, d. 1985; Boganda Day, Central African Republic; Memorial Day, Madagascar.

30 Fri: Warren Beatty, b. 1937; Celine Dion, b. 1968; Beau Brummell, d. 1840; Shouter Liberation Day, Trinidad & Tobago.

31 Sat: René Descartes, b. 1596; Ewan McGregor, b. 1971; Charlotte Brontë, d. 1855; Freedom Day, Malta.

Weather forecast for March: Some areas of Britain may see rain of varying amounts while others may remain dry from time to time. There will be some sunshine in certain places, particularly where the clouds break, as well as a risk of thunder and maybe fog. Where trees start blowing about, it will be windy. Snow, sleet and hail are also possible but may not happen at all. Temperatures will be around, above or below normal. It will generally be dark at night, but lighter by day.

APRIL

1 Sun: Debbie Reynolds, b. 1932; Eleanor of Aquitaine, d. 1204; Marvin Gaye, d. 1984.

2 Mon: Charlemagne, b. AD 742; Linford Christie, b. 1960; Georges Pompidou, d. 1974; Malvinas Day, Argentina.

3 Tues: Eddie Murphy, b. 1961; Johannes Brahms, d. 1897; Graham Greene d. 1991.

4 Wed: David Blaine, b. 1973; Oliver Goldsmith, d. 1774; Liberation Day, Hungary.

5 Thurs: Agnetha Faltskog, b. 1950; Howard Hughes, d. 1976; Tomb Sweeping Day, Macau.

6 Fri: John Betjeman, b. 1906; Richard I, d. 1199; Chakri Day, Thailand.

7 Sat: William Wordsworth, b. 1770; Russell Crowe, b. 1964; Dick Turpin, d. 1739; Women's Day, Mozambique.

8 Sun: Vivienne Westwood, b. 1941; Elisha Graves Otis (inventor of the lift), d. 1861; Pablo Picasso, d. 1973.

9 Mon: Rachel Stevens, b. 1978; Frank Lloyd Wright, d. 1959; Valour Day, Philippines.

10 Tues: Gloria Hunniford, b. 1940; Lesley Garrett, b. 1955; Evelyn Waugh, d. 1966.

11 Wed: Jeremy Clarkson, b. 1960; Llywelyn ap Iorwerth, Prince of Wales, d. 1240; Heroes' Day, Costa Rica.

12 Thurs: Bobby Moore, b. 1941; David Cassidy, b. 1950; Joe Louis, d. 1981.

13 Fri: Frank Winfield Woolworth, b. 1852; Peter Davison, b. 1951; Tewodros II, Emperor of Ethiopia, d. 1868; New Year's Day, Cambodia.

14 Sat: Sarah Michelle Gellar, b. 1977; George Frederick Handel, d. 1759; Pan American Day, Honduras.

15 Sun: Emma Thompson, b. 1959; Katy Hill, b. 1971; Tommy Cooper, d. 1984; Father Damien Day, Hawaii.

16 Mon: Freddie Ljungberg, b. 1977; Bertram Mills, d. 1938; New Year's Day, Burma.

17 Tues: Victoria Beckham, b. 1974; Benjamin Franklin, d. 1790; Independence Day, Syria; National Health Day, Kiribati.

18 Wed: Lucrezia Borgia, b. 1480; Albert Einstein, d. 1955; Benny Hill, d. 1992; Independence Day, Zimbabwe.

19 Thurs: Rivaldo, b. 1972; Charles Darwin, d. 1882; Frankie Howerd, d. 1992; Landing of the 33 Patriots Day, Uruguay; National High Five Day, USA.

20 Fri: Adolf Hitler, b. 1889; Luther Vandross, b. 1951; Canaletto, d. 1768.

21 Sat: Alistair MacLean, b. 1922; Henry VII, d. 1509; Tiradentes Day, Brazil.

22 Sun: Henry Fielding, b. 1707; Jack Nicholson, b. 1937; Richard Trevithick, d. 1833; Discovery Day, Brazil.

23 Mon: William Shakespeare, b. 1564; Otto Preminger, d. 1986; Children's Day, Turkey.

24 Tues: Barbra Streisand, b. 1942; Sachin Tendulkar, b. 1973; Daniel Defoe, d. 1731; Genocide Remembrance Day, Armenia.

25 Wed: Fiona Bruce, b. 1964; Anders Celsius (inventor of Centigrade thermometer), d. 1744; Sinai Day, Egypt.

26 Thurs: Leonardo da Vinci, b. 1452; Broderick Crawford, d. 1986; Union Day, Tanzania.

27 Fri: Sheena Easton, b. 1959; King Ardashir III of Persia, d. AD 630; Independence Day, Sierra Leone.

28 Sat: Saddam Hussein, b. 1937; John Daly, b. 1966; Fuad I of Egypt, d. 1936; Bounty Day, Pitcairn; Day of Nature, Japan.

29 Sun: Michelle Pfeiffer, b. 1958; Alfred Hitchcock, d. 1980; Green Day, Japan.

30 Mon: Bobby Vee, b. 1943; Edouard Manet, d. 1883; Vappu Day, Finland.

Weather forecast for April: Some areas of Britain may see rain of varying amounts while others may remain dry from time to time. There will be some sunshine in certain places, particularly where the clouds break, as well as a risk of thunder and maybe fog. Where trees start blowing about, it will be windy. Snow, sleet and hail are also possible but may not happen at all. Temperatures will be around, above or below normal. It will generally be dark at night, but lighter by day.

•

MAY

1 Tues: Calamity Jane, b. 1852; Ayrton Senna, d. 1994; Day of the People, Kazakhstan.

2 Wed: Catherine the Great, b. 1729; David Beckham, b. 1975; J. Edgar Hoover, d. 1972; National Education Day, Indonesia.

3 Thurs: Niccolò Machiavelli, b. 1469; Ben Elton, b. 1959; Barbara Castle, d. 2002; Constitution Day, Poland.

4 Fri: Audrey Hepburn, b. 1929; Diana Dors, d. 1984; People's Day, Japan; Liberty Day, Netherlands.

5 Sat: Craig David, b. 1981; Napoleon Bonaparte, d. 1821; Cinco de Mayo, Mexico.

6 Sun: George Clooney, b. 1961; Marlene Dietrich, d. 1992; Corregidor Day, Philippines; Working Day, Ukraine.

7 Mon: Robert Browning, b. 1812; Eva Peron, b. 1919; Douglas Fairbanks Jr., d. 2000; Radio and Television Day, Bulgaria.

8 Tues: H from Steps, b. 1976; Paul Gauguin. d. 1903; Liberation Day, France.

9 Wed: Glenda Jackson, b. 1936; Billy Joel, b. 1949; Aldo Moro, d. 1978; Liberation Day, Channel Islands.

10 Thurs: Fred Astaire, b. 1899; Bono, b. 1960; Joan Crawford, d. 1977; Constitution Day, Micronesia; Tin Hau's Day, China.

11 Fri: Salvador Dali, b. 1904; Kim Philby, d. 1988; National Day, Laos.

12 Sat: Florence Nightingale, b. 1820; Katharine Hepburn, b. 1907; Pope Silvester II, d. 1003.

13 Sun: Daphne du Maurier, b. 1907; Stevie Wonder, b. 1950; Gary Cooper, d. 1961; Rotuma Day, Fiji.

14 Mon: Martine McCutcheon, b. 1976; August Strindberg, d. 1912; Kamuzu Day, Malawi.

15 Tues: Sophie Raworth, b. 1968; Rita Hayworth, d. 1987; Independence Day, Israel.

16 Wed: Olga Korbut, b. 1955; Jim Henson, d. 1990; Royal Ploughing Day, Cambodia.

17 Thurs: Andrea Corr, b. 1974; Donald Coggan, Archbishop of Canterbury, d. 2000; Constitution Day, Norway.

18 Fri: Toyah Willcox, b. 1958; Rupert, King of Germany, d. 1410; Las Piedras Day, Uruguay.

19 Sat: Ho Chi Minh, b. 1890; Ann Boleyn, d. 1536; Flag Day, Finland.

20 Sun: Cher, b. 1946; Christopher Columbus, d. 1506; Popular Movement Day, Zaire.

21 Mon: Alexander Pope, b. 1688; Henry VI, d. 1471; Navy Day, Chile.

22 Tues: Naomi Campbell, b. 1970; Constantine the Great, d. AD 337; Sovereign Day, Haiti.

23 Wed: Joan Collins, b. 1933; Bonnie and Clyde, d. 1934; Vesak Day, South Korea.

24 Thurs: Bob Dylan, b. 1941; Duke Ellington, d. 1974; Culture Day, Bulgaria; Independence Battle Day, Ecuador.

25 Fri: Ian McKellen, b. 1939; The Venerable Bede, d. AD 735; Revolution Day, Argentina.

26 Sat: John Wayne, b. 1907; Samuel Pepys, d. 1703; Independence Day, Guyana.

27 Sun: Vincent Price, b. 1911; Christopher Lee, b. 1922; John Calvin, d. 1564; Mother's Day, Bolivia.

28 Mon: John the Fearless; Duke of Burgundy, b. 1371; Kylie Minogue, b. 1968; Eric Morecambe, d. 1984; Republic Day, Azerbaijan.

29 Tues: John F. Kennedy, b. 1917; Noel Gallagher, b. 1967; Sir Humphry Davy, d. 1829; Democracy Day, Nigeria.

30 Wed: Steven Gerrard, b. 1980; Joan of Arc, d. 1431; Indian Arrival Day, Trinidad & Tobago.

31 Thurs: Brooke Shields, b. 1965; Jack Dempsey, d. 1983; Regiment Day, Brunei; Prince Albert Day, Monaco.

Weather forecast for May: Some areas of Britain may see rain of varying amounts while others may remain dry from time to time. There will be some sunshine in certain places, particularly where the clouds break, as well as a risk of thunder and maybe fog. Where trees start blowing about, it will be windy. Snow, sleet and hail are also possible but may not happen at all. Temperatures will be around, above or below normal. It will generally be dark at night, but lighter by day.

•

JUNE

1 Fri: Alanis Morissette, b. 1974; Lizzie Borden, d. 1927; Madaraka Day, Kenya.

2 Sat: Edward Elgar, b. 1857; Rex Harrison, d. 1990; Republic Day, Italy.

3 Sun: Suzi Quatro, b. 1950; Wasim Akram, b. 1966; Robert Morley, d. 1992.

4 Mon: George III, b. 1738; Angelina Jolie, b. 1975; Casanova, d. 1798; National Day, Tonga.

5 Tues: Ross Noble, b. 1976; Ronald Reagan, d. 2004; Independence Day, Seychelles.

6 Wed: David Blunkett, b. 1947; Carl Jung, d. 1961; National Day, Sweden.

7 Thurs: Tom Jones, b. 1940; the artist occasionally known as Prince, b. 1958; Robert the Bruce, d. 1329; Union Dissolution Day, Norway.

8 Fri: Joan Rivers, b. 1933; Mick Hucknall, b. 1960; Edward, the Black Prince, d. 1376.

9 Sat: George Stephenson, b. 1781; Johnny Depp, b. 1963; Sybil Thorndike, d. 1976.

10 Sun: Elizabeth Hurley, b. 1965; George I, d. 1727; National Day, Portugal.

11 Mon: John Constable, b. 1776; John Wayne, d. 1979; Evacuation Day, Libya.

12 Tues: Anne Frank, b. 1929; William Collins, d. 1759; Independence Day, Philippines.

13 Wed: Mary Whitehouse, b. 1910; Kathy Burke, b. 1964; Alexander the Great, d. 323 BC.

14 Thurs: Donald Trump, b. 1946; Boy George, b. 1961; John Logie Baird, d. 1946; Mother's Day, Afghanistan.

15 Fri: Noddy Holder, b. 1946; Wat Tyler, d. 1381; Mangaia Gospel Day, Cook Islands.

16 Sat: Stan Laurel, b. 1890; Phil Mickelson, b. 1970; Lord Reith, d. 1971; Youth Day, South Africa.

17 Sun: Venus Williams, b. 1980; John III Sobieski, King of Poland, d. 1696; Republic Day, Iceland.

18 Mon: Paul McCartney, b. 1942; Roald Amundsen, d. 1928; Chemist's Day, Brazil.

19 Tues: Boris Johnson, b. 1964; J. M. Barrie, d. 1937; Artigas Day, Uruguay.

20 Wed: Nicole Kidman, b. 1967; William IV, d. 1837; Flag Day, Argentina.

21 Thurs: Ray Davies, b. 1944; Prince William, b. 1982; Inigo Jones, d. 1652; Ullortuneg (National Day), Greenland.

22 Fri: Cyndi Lauper, b. 1953; Judy Garland, d. 1969; Anti-Fascism Day, Croatia.

23 Sat: Zinedine Zidane, b. 1972; Buster Merryfield, d. 1999; Johannus Day, Finland; Grand Duke Day, Luxembourg; Ligo Day, Latvia.

24 Sun: Mick Fleetwood, b. 1942; Tony Hancock, d. 1968; St. John's Day, Andorra; Carabobo Day, Venezuela.

25 Mon: Ricky Gervais, b. 1961; General George Custer, d. 1876; Independence Day, Croatia.

26 Tues: Paolo Maldini, b. 1968; Sandy Powell, d. 1982; Independence Day, Madagascar.

27 Wed: Alan Coren, b. 1938; Jack Lemmon, d. 2001; Independence Day, Djibouti.

28 Thurs: Henry VIII, b. 1491; John Inman, b. 1935; Victor Trumper, d. 1915.

29 Fri: Katherine Jenkins, b. 1980; Fatty Arbuckle, d. 1933; Jayne Mansfield, d. 1967; Independence Day, Seychelles.

30 Sat: Mike Tyson, b. 1966; Aztec emperor Montezuma II, d. 1520; Army Day, Guatemala.

Weather forecast for June: Some areas of Britain may see rain of varying amounts while others may remain dry from time to time. There will be some sunshine in certain places, particularly where the clouds break, as well as a risk of thunder and maybe fog. Where trees start blowing about, it will be windy. Snow, sleet and hail are also possible but may not happen at all. Temperatures will be around, above or below normal. It will generally be dark at night, but lighter by day.

•

JULY

1 Sun: Pamela Anderson, b. 1967; Erik Satie, d. 1925; Freedom Day, Suriname; Independence Day, Burundi; Civil Servants' Day, Hungary.

2 Mon: Peter Kay, b. 1973; Nostradamus, d. 1566; Family Day, Lesotho.

3 Tues: Tom Cruise, b. 1962; Jim Morrison, d. 1971; Unity Day, Zambia.

4 Wed: Gina Lollobrigida, b. 1927; Marie Curie, d. 1934, Barry White, d. 2003; Liberation Day, Rwanda.

5 Thurs: Cecil Rhodes, b. 1853; Thomas Stamford Raffles, d. 1826; Tynwald Day, Isle of Man.

6 Fri: Tsar Nicholas I of Russia, b. 1796; Louis Armstrong, d. 1971; Statehood Day, Lithuania; Jan Hus Day, Czech Republic; Independence Day, Malawi.

7 Sat: Ringo Starr, b. 1940; Arthur Conan Doyle, d. 1930; Farmers' Day, Tanzania; Fishermen's Day, Marshall Islands.

8 Sun: Marty Feldman, b. 1933; Percy Bysshe Shelley, d. 1822; Vivien Leigh, d. 1967.

9 Mon: O.J. Simpson, b. 1947; Edmund Burke, d. 1797; Independence Day, Argentina.

10 Tues: Virginia Wade, b. 1945; William the Silent, Prince of Orange, d. 1584; Independence Day, Bahamas.

11 Wed: Giorgio Armani, b. 1934; George Gershwin, d. 1937; Revolution Day, Mongolia.

12 Thurs: Gareth Gates, b. 1984; Desiderius Erasmus, d. 1536; Independence Day, São Tomé e Principe.

13 Fri: Julius Agricola b. AD 40; Ernö Rubik (inventor of Rubik's Cube), b. 1944; Arnold Schoenberg, d. 1951.

14 Sat: Sue Lawley, b. 1946; Adlai Stevenson, d. 1965; Bastille Day, France.

15 Sun: Iris Murdoch, b. 1919; Linda Ronstadt, b. 1946; General Tom Thumb (professional dwarf), d. 1883; President's Day, Botswana.

16 Mon: Joshua Reynolds, b. 1723; Ginger Rogers, b. 1911; Josiah Spode, d. 1827.

17 Tues: David Hasselhoff, b. 1952; Fern Britton, b. 1957; Billie Holiday, d. 1959; Rivera Day, Puerto Rico.

18 Wed: Richard Branson, b. 1950; Jane Austen, d. 1817; Eruption Day, Montserrat.

19 Thurs: Brian May, b. 1947; Thomas Cook, d. 1892; Sandinista Day, Nicaragua.

20 Fri: Diana Rigg, b. 1938; Pope Leo XIII, d. 1903; Independence Day, Colombia.

21 Sat: Robin Williams, b. 1952; Robert Burns, d. 1796; National Day, Belgium.

22 Sun: Bonnie Langford, b. 1964; John Dillinger, d. 1934; Liberation Day, Poland.

23 Mon: Slash from Guns 'n' Roses, b. 1965; Monica Lewinsky, b. 1973; Montgomery Clift, d. 1966; Hurricane Supplication Day, Virgin Islands.

24 Tues: Jennifer Lopez, b. 1970; Peter Sellers, d. 1980; Bolivar Day, Venezuela.

25 Wed: Matt LeBlanc, b. 1967; Samuel Taylor Coleridge, d. 1834; Guanacaste Day, Costa Rica.

26 Thurs: Mick Jagger, b. 1937; Offa, King of Mercia, d. AD 796; Independence Day, Maldives.

27 Fri: Allan Border, b. 1955; Bob Hope, d. 2003; Barbosa Day, Puerto Rico.

28 Sat: Beatrix Potter, b. 1866; Thomas Cromwell, d. 1540; Independence Day, Peru.

29 Sun: Fernando Alonso, b. 1981; Umberto I of Italy, d. 1900; Asalacha Bucha Day, Thailand; Olavsøka National Day, Faroe Islands.

30 Mon: Arnold Schwarzenegger, b. 1947; Thomas Gray, d. 1771; Khao Phansa Day, Thailand; Enthronement Day, Morocco.

31 Tues: Jonathan Dimbleby, b. 1944; J.K. Rowling, b. 1965; Ignatius Loyola, d. 1556.

Weather forecast for July: Some areas of Britain may see rain of varying amounts while others may remain dry from time to time. There will be some sunshine in certain places, particularly where the clouds break, as well as a risk of thunder and maybe fog. Where trees start blowing about, it will be windy. Snow, sleet and hail are also possible but may not happen at all. Temperatures will be around, above or below normal. It will generally be dark at night, but lighter by day.

AUGUST

1 Wed: Emperor Claudius, b. 10 BC; Louis VI of France, d. 1137; Confederation Day, Switzerland; Emancipation Day, Jamaica.

2 Thurs: Peter O'Toole, b. 1932; Wild Bill Hickok, d. 1876; Virgin of the Angels Day, Costa Rica; Ilinden Day, FYP Macedonia.

3 Fri: King Haakon VII of Norway, b. 1872; Gina G, b. 1970; Richard Arkwright, d. 1792; Armed Forces Day, Equatorial Guinea.

4 Sat: Billy Bob Thornton, b. 1955; Simon de Montfort, d. 1265; Victor Mature, d. 1999.

5 Sun: Pete Burns, b. 1959; Richard Burton, d. 1984; Independence Day, Burkina Faso.

6 Mon: Barbara Windsor, b. 1937; Pope Paul VI, d. 1978; Emancipation Day, Bahamas.

7 Tues: Alexei Sayle, b. 1952; Oliver Hardy, d. 1957; Boyaca Day, Colombia; Commerce Day, India.

8 Wed: Dustin Hoffman, b. 1937; Roger Federer, b. 1981; Barbara Bel Geddes, d. 2005; Queen Silvia's Name Day, Sweden.

9 Thurs: Whitney Houston, b. 1963; Joe Orton, d. 1967; National Day, Singapore.

10 Fri: Kate O'Mara, b. 1939; Ferdinand VI of Spain, d. 1759; Independence Day, Ecuador.

11 Sat: Joe Jackson, b. 1954; Wilfred the Hairy, Count of Barcelona, d. 897; Jackson Pollock, d. 1956; Valentine's Day, Taiwan.

12 Sun: Mark Knopfler, b. 1949; Pete Sampras, b. 1971; George Stephenson, d. 1848.

13 Mon: Alan Shearer, b. 1970; H.G. Wells, d. 1946; Women's Day, Tunisia.

14 Tues: Halle Berry, b. 1968; J.B. Priestley, d. 1984; Independence Day, Pakistan.

15 Wed: Princess Anne, b. 1950; Macbeth, King of Scotland, d. 1057; National Day, Liechtenstein.

16 Thurs: Madonna, b. 1958; Elvis Presley, d. 1977; Independence Day, Cyprus.

17 Fri: Thierry Henry, b. 1977; Frederick the Great of Prussia, d. 1786; San Martin's Day, Argentina.

18 Sat: Max Factor, b. 1904; Genghis Khan, d. 1227; Independence Day, Afghanistan.

19 Sun: Billy J. Kramer, b. 1943; Bill Clinton, b. 1946; Alastair Sim, d. 1976; National Aviation Day, USA.

20 Mon: Robert Plant, b. 1948; Jessie Matthews, d. 1981; Constitution Day, Hungary.

21 Tues: Princess Margaret, b. 1930; Chantelle, b. 1983; Leon Trotsky, d. 1940; Ninoy Aquino Day, Philippines.

22 Wed: Norman Schwarzkopf, b. 1934; Steve Davis, b. 1957; Jomo Kenyatta, d. 1978.

23 Thurs: Keith Moon, b. 1946; Oscar Hammerstein II, d. 1960; Liberation Day, Romania.

24 Fri: Yasser Arafat, b. 1929; Stephen Fry, b. 1957; Colonel Thomas Blood, d. 1680; Flag Day, Liberia.

25 Sat: Claudia Schiffer, b. 1970; James Watt, d. 1819; Independence Day, Uruguay.

26 Sun: Macaulay Culkin, b. 1980; Frans Hals, d. 1666, Charles
Lindbergh, d. 1974; Heroes' Day, Namibia.

27 Mon: Mother Teresa, b. 1910; Bernhard Langer, b. 1957;
Titian, d. 1576; Independence Day, Moldova.

28 Tues: David Soul, b. 1944; Shania Twain, b. 1965;
King Boris III of Bulgaria, d. 1943; Liberation Day, Hong Kong.

29 Wed: Ingrid Bergman, b. 1915; Byzantine Emperor Basil I,
d. AD 886; Slovak National Uprising Day, Slovakia.

30 Thurs: Cameron Diaz, b. 1972; Cleopatra, d. 30 BC; Rose of Lima
Day, Peru.

31 Fri: Caligula, b. AD 12; Richard Gere, b. 1949; Rocky Marciano,
d. 1969; Pashtunistan Day, Afghanistan; Merdeka Day, Malaysia;
National Language Day, Moldova.

Weather forecast for August: Some areas of Britain may see rain of
varying amounts while others may remain dry from time to time.
There will be some sunshine in certain places, particularly where
the clouds break, as well as a risk of thunder and maybe fog.
Where trees start blowing about, it will be windy. Snow, sleet and
hail are also possible but may not happen at all. Temperatures will
be around, above or below normal. It will generally be dark at
night, but lighter by day.

•

SEPTEMBER

1 Sat: Conway Twitty, b. 1933; Siegfried Sassoon, d. 1967;
Revolution Day, Libya; Knowledge Day, Latvia.

2 Sun: Lennox Lewis, b. 1965; Thomas Telford, d. 1834; National
Day, Vietnam.

3 Mon: Fearne Cotton, b. 1982; Oliver Cromwell, d. 1658;
Fair Day, Luxembourg; St Marinus' Day, San Marino.

4 Tues: Wanli, Emperor of China, b. 1563; Beyonce Knowles,
b. 1981; Edvard Grieg, d. 1907.

5 Wed: Louis XIV of France, b. 1638; Raquel Welch, b. 1940;
Douglas Bader, d. 1982; Teacher's Day, India.

6 Thurs: Macy Gray, b. 1970; Suleiman the Magnificent, d. 1566;
Defence Day, Pakistan; Somhlolo Day, Swaziland.

7 Fri: Chrissie Hynde, b. 1951; C.B. Fry, d. 1956; Independence Day,
Brazil.

8 Sat: Pink, b. 1979; Richard Strauss, d. 1949; Our Lady of Victory
Day, Malta.

9 Sun: Hugh Grant, b. 1960; William the Conqueror, d. 1087;
Liberation Day, Bulgaria.

10 Mon: Arnold Palmer, b. 1929; Colin Firth, b. 1960; Charles Cruft
(founder of the dog show), d. 1938; Day of the Child, Honduras.

11 Tues: Franz Beckenbauer, b. 1945; Moby, b. 1965;
Nikita Khrushchev, d. 1971; National Day, Catalonia.

12 Wed: Jesse Owens, b. 1913; Anthony Perkins, d. 1992;
Johnny Cash, d. 2003; National Day, Cape Verde.

13 Thurs: Carol Barnes, b. 1944; Shane Warne, b. 1969;
Philip II of Spain, d. 1598.

14 Fri: Morten Harket, b. 1959; Princess Grace of Monaco, d. 1982;
San Jacinto Day, Nicaragua.

15 Sat: Graham Taylor, b. 1944; Isambard Kingdom Brunel, d. 1859; Veneration Day, Japan.

16 Sun: Lauren Bacall, b. 1924; Tomás de Torquemada, d. 1498; Independence Day, Papua New Guinea.

17 Mon: Francis Chichester, b. 1901; Damon Hill, b. 1960; Tobias George Smollett, d. 1771; Von Steuben Day, USA.

18 Tues: Dr Samuel Johnson, b. 1709; Jimi Hendrix, d. 1970; Victory of Uprona Day, Burundi; Respect for the Aged Day, Japan.

19 Wed: Jeremy Irons, b. 1948; Jarvis Cocker, b. 1963; Roy Kinnear, d. 1988; Independence Day, Saint Kitts & Nevis.

20 Thurs: Sophia Loren, b. 1934; Jean Sibelius, d. 1957; Brian Clough, d. 2004.

21 Fri: Leonard Cohen, b. 1934; Virgil, d. 19 BC; Independence Day, Belize.

22 Sat: Anne of Cleves, b. 1515; Billie Piper, b. 1982; Irving Berlin, d. 1989; Republic Day, Mali; Baltic Unity Day, Latvia.

23 Sun: Bruce Springsteen, b. 1949; Sigmund Freud, d. 1939; National Day, Saudi Arabia.

24 Mon: Gerry Marsden, b. 1942; Pepin the Short, King of the Franks, d. 768; Mercedes Day, Dominican Republic.

25 Tues: Michael Douglas, b. 1944; Catherine Zeta Jones, b. 1969; Walter Pidgeon, d. 1984; Assembly Day, Rwanda; Heritage Day, South Africa.

26 Wed: Olivia Newton-John, b. 1948; Béla Bartók, d. 1945; National Day, Yemen.

27 Thurs: Alvin Stardust, b. 1942; Gracie Fields, d. 1979; True Cross Day, Ethiopia.

28 Fri: Michelangelo, b. 1573; Gwyneth Paltrow, b. 1972;
Harpo Marx, d. 1964; Teacher's Day, Taiwan.

29 Sat: Greer Garson, b. 1904; W.H. Auden, d. 1973;
Boqueron Battle Day, Paraguay.

30 Sun: Martina Hingis, b. 1980; James Dean, d. 1955;
Independence Day, Botswana.

Weather forecast for September: Some areas of Britain may see rain
of varying amounts while others may remain dry from time to
time. There will be some sunshine in certain places, particularly
where the clouds break, as well as a risk of thunder and maybe
fog. Where trees start blowing about, it will be windy. Snow, sleet
and hail are also possible but may not happen at all. Temperatures
will be around, above or below normal. It will generally be dark at
night, but lighter by day.

•

OCTOBER

1 Mon: Julie Andrews, b. 1935; Edwin Landseer, d. 1873;
Independence Day, Nigeria.

2 Tues: Richard III, b. 1452; Sting, b. 1951; Rock Hudson, d. 1985;
Independence Day, Guinea.

3 Wed: Gwen Stefani, b. 1969; Malcolm Sargent, d. 1967;
Morazan Day, Honduras.

4 Thurs: Ann Widdecombe, b. 1947; Graham Chapman, d. 1989;
Independence Day, Lesotho.

5 Fri: Kate Winslet, b. 1975; Nelson Riddle, d. 1985; Sports Day,
Lesotho.

6 Sat: Le Corbusier, b. 1887; Charles the Bald, Holy Roman
Emperor, d. AD 877; Armed Forces Day, Egypt.

7 Sun: Vladimir Putin, b. 1952; Simon Cowell, b. 1959; Clarence Birdseye, d. 1956.

8 Mon: Ardal O'Hanlon, b. 1965; Henry Fielding, d. 1754; Puerto Rican Friendship Day, Virgin Islands; Spanishness Day, Chile.

9 Tues: Steve Ovett, b. 1955; Gabriel Fallopius, d. 1562; National Dignity Day, Peru; Physical Fitness Day, Japan; Alphabet Day, South Korea.

10 Wed: David Lee Roth, b. 1954; Edith Piaf, d. 1963; Independence War Day, Cuba; Health Day, Japan.

11 Thurs: Bobby Charlton, b. 1937; Dawn French, b. 1957; Jean Cocteau, d. 1963.

12 Fri: Luciano Pavarotti, b. 1935; Edith Cavell, d. 1915; National Day, Spain.

13 Sat: Margaret Thatcher, b. 1925; Marie Osmond, b. 1959; Henry Irving, d. 1905.

14 Sun: Cliff Richard, b. 1940; Bing Crosby, d. 1977; Founders' Day, Zaire; Svetitskhovloba, Georgia.

15 Mon: P.G. Wodehouse, b. 1881; Sarah Ferguson, b. 1959; Hermann Goering, d. 1946; White Cane Safety Day, USA.

16 Tues: Angela Lansbury, b. 1925; Flea from Red Hot Chili Peppers, b. 1962; Marie Antoinette, d. 1793.

17 Wed: Peter Stringfellow, b. 1940; Frederic Chopin, d. 1849; Dessalines Day, Haiti; Mother's Day, Malawi.

18 Thurs: Martina Navratilova, b. 1956; Jean-Claude Van Damme, b. 1960; Elizabeth Arden, d. 1966.

19 Fri: Evander Holyfield, b. 1962; King John, d. 1216; Jacqueline Du Pré, d. 1987; Mother Teresa Day, Albania.

20 Sat: Snoop Dogg, b. 1971; Bud Flanagan, d. 1968;
Kenyatta Day, Kenya.

21 Sun: Peter Mandelson, b. 1953; David Campese, b. 1962;
Horatio Nelson, d. 1805; Compact Day, Marshall Islands;
Antilles Day, Curaçao.

22 Mon: Franz Liszt, b. 1811; Shaggy, b. 1968; Paul Cézanne,
d. 1906.

23 Tues: Pelé, b. 1940; Al Jolson, d. 1950; Chulalongkorn Day,
Thailand.

24 Wed: Wayne Rooney, b. 1985; Christian Dior, d. 1957;
Independence Day, Zambia.

25 Thurs: Helen Reddy, b. 1942; Geoffrey Chaucer, d. 1400;
Restoration Day, Taiwan.

26 Fri: François Mitterand, b. 1916; Alma Cogan, d. 1966;
Angam Day, Nauru; Government Day, Rwanda.

27 Sat: John Cleese, b. 1939; Athelstan I of England, d. AD 939;
Naming Day, Zaire.

28 Sun: Bill Gates, b. 1955; John Locke, d. 1704; Ochi Day, Greece.

29 Mon: Winona Ryder, b. 1971; Gustav V of Sweden, d. 1950;
Republic Day, Turkey.

30 Tues: Michael Winner, b. 1935; Diego Maradona, b. 1960;
Barnes Wallis, d. 1979.

31 Wed: John Keats, b. 1795; Jimmy Savile, b. 1926; Harry Houdini,
d. 1926.

Weather forecast for October: Some areas of Britain may see rain of
varying amounts while others may remain dry from time to time.
There will be some sunshine in certain places, particularly where

the clouds break, as well as a risk of thunder and maybe fog. Where trees start blowing about, it will be windy. Snow, sleet and hail are also possible but may not happen at all. Temperatures will be around, above or below normal. It will generally be dark at night, but lighter by day.

•

NOVEMBER

1 Thurs: Gary Player, b. 1975; Phil Silvers, d. 1985; Revolution Day, Algeria.

2 Fri: Ken Rosewall, b. 1934; George Bernard Shaw, d. 1950; Day of the Dead, Mexico; Memorial Day, Brazil; Arrival of Indentured Labourers Day, Mauritius.

3 Sat: Adam Ant, b. 1954; Henri Matisse, d. 1954; Day of Trees, Samoa; Culture Day, Japan.

4 Sun: P. Diddy, b. 1969; Felix Mendelssohn, d. 1847; St. Charles' Day, Andorra.

5 Mon: Lester Piggott, b. 1935; Bryan Adams, b. 1959; Robert Maxwell, d. 1991; Cry of Independence Day, El Salvador.

6 Tues: Frank Carson, b. 1926; Nell McAndrew, b. 1973; Peter Ilyich Tchaikovsky, d. 1893; Constitution Day, Tajikistan.

7 Wed: Su Pollard, b. 1949; Sharleen Spiteri, b. 1967; Steve McQueen, d. 1980.

8 Thurs: Christiaan Barnard, b. 1922; Joe Cole, b. 1981; John Milton, d. 1674.

9 Fri: Delta Goodrem, b. 1984; Charles de Gaulle, d. 1970; National Reconciliation Day, Tajikistan; Iqbal Day, Pakistan.

10 Sat: Screaming Lord Sutch, b. 1940; Tim Rice, b. 1944; Gordon Richards, d. 1986.

11 Sun: Demi Moore, b. 1962; Ned Kelly, d. 1880; Wasteland Day, Angola.

12 Mon: Tonya Harding, b. 1970; King Canute, d. 1035; Independence Day, Comoros; Santa Cruz Day, Timor.

13 Tues: Robert Louis Stevenson, b. 1850; Whoopi Goldberg, b. 1955; Henry the Navigator, d. 1460.

14 Wed: Claude Monet, b. 1840; Prince Charles, b. 1948; Nell Gwyn, d. 1687.

15 Thurs: William Pitt the Elder, b. 1708; Petula Clark, b. 1934; John Le Mesurier, d. 1983; Day of Peace, Côte d'Ivoire.

16 Fri: Emperor Tiberius, b. 42 BC; Frank Bruno, b. 1961; Perkin Warbeck, d. 1499; Language Day, Iceland.

17 Sat: Jonathan Ross, b. 1960; François-Auguste Rodin, d. 1917; Struggle for Liberty and Democracy Day, Czech Republic.

18 Sun: Kim Wilde, b. 1960; Marcel Proust, d. 1922; Vertieres Day, Haiti.

19 Mon: Calvin Klein, b. 1942; Franz Schubert, d. 1828; Garifuna Day, Belize; Prince Rainier Day, Monaco.

20 Tues: Joe Walsh, b. 1947; Bo Derek, b. 1956; Maud, Queen of Norway, d. 1938; Zumbi Day, Brazil.

21 Wed: Voltaire, b. 1694; Björk, b. 1965; Henry Purcell, d. 1695; Repentance Day, Germany.

22 Thurs: Boris Becker, b. 1967; Mae West, d. 1980; Independence Day, Lebanon.

23 Fri: Boris Karloff, b. 1887; Zoe Ball, b. 1970; Dr Hawley Harvey Crippen, d. 1910; Rudolf Maister Day, Slovenia.

24 Sat: Ian Botham, b. 1955; Freddie Mercury, d. 1991; New Regime Day, Zaire.

25 Sun: Catherine of Braganza, b. 1638; George Best, d. 2005; Independence Day, Suriname; National Day, Bosnia & Herzegovina.

26 Mon: Tina Turner, b. 1938; John Selwyn Gummer, b. 1939; Michael Bentine, d. 1996; Proclamation Day, Mongolia.

27 Tues: Ernie Wise, b. 1925; Bruce Lee, b. 1940; Horace, d. 8 BC.

28 Wed: Anna Nicole Smith, b. 1967; Enid Blyton, d. 1968; Independence Day, Mauritania.

29 Thurs: Busby Berkeley, b. 1895; Graham Hill, d. 1975; Coors Day, Yemen.

30 Fri: Billy Idol, b. 1955; Gary Lineker, b. 1960; Cary Grant, d. 1986; Bonifacio Day, Philippines.

Weather forecast for November: Some areas of Britain may see rain of varying amounts while others may remain dry from time to time. There will be some sunshine in certain places, particularly where the clouds break, as well as a risk of thunder and maybe fog. Where trees start blowing about, it will be windy. Snow, sleet and hail are also possible but may not happen at all. Temperatures will be around, above or below normal. It will generally be dark at night, but lighter by day.

DECEMBER

1 Sat: Bette Midler, b. 1945; Pope Leo X, d. 1521; Youth Day, Portugal.

2 Sun: Gianni Versace, b. 1946; Britney Spears, b. 1981; Philip Larkin, d. 1985; National Day, Laos.

3 Mon: Mel Smith, b. 1952; Franz Klammer, b. 1953; Oswald Mosley, d. 1980.

4 Tues: Ronnie Corbett, b. 1930; Benjamin Britten, d. 1976; Frank Zappa, d. 1993; Navy Day, India.

5 Wed: Walt Disney, b. 1901; Little Richard, b. 1932; Wolfgang Amadeus Mozart, d. 1791; Krampus Day, Austria.

6 Thurs: Henry VI, b. 1421; Roy Orbison, d. 1988; Independence Day, Finland.

7 Fri: Marie Tussaud, b. 1761; John Terry, b. 1980; Cicero, d. 43 BC.

8 Sat: James Galway, b. 1939; Sinead O'Connor, b. 1966; John Lennon, d. 1980; Day of the Student, Bulgaria.

9 Sun: Donny Osmond, b. 1957; Edith Sitwell, d. 1964; Independence Day, Tanzania.

10 Mon: Kenneth Branagh, b. 1960; Leopold I, King of the Belgians, d. 1865; Settlers' Day, Namibia.

11 Tues: Cliff Michelmore, b. 1919; Sam Cooke, d. 1964; Republic Day, Burkina Faso.

12 Wed: Jasper Conran, b. 1959; Darius the Bastard, King of Persia, d. 404 BC; Neutrality Day, Turkmenistan; Independence Day, Kenya.

13 Thurs: John Francome, b. 1952; Dr Samuel Johnson, d. 1784; Soot Sweeping Day, Japan.

14 Fri: George VI, b. 1895; Michael Owen, b. 1979; George Washington, d. 1799.

15 Sat: Nero, b. AD 37; Frankie Dettori, b. 1970; Isaak Walton, d. 1683.

16 Sun: Jack Hobbs, b. 1882; W. Somerset Maugham, d. 1965; Covenant Day, South Africa.

17 Mon: Paula Radcliffe, b. 1973; Queen Nzinga of Ndongo and Matamba, d. 1663; Sow Day, Orkney.

18 Tues: Christina Aguilera, b. 1980; Dorothy L. Sayers, d. 1957; Independence Day, Niger.

19 Wed: Leonid Brezhnev, b. 1906; Syd Little, b. 1942; Emily Brontë, d. 1848.

20 Thurs: Uri Geller, b. 1946; Billy Bragg, b. 1958; Ignatius, Bishop of Antioch d. 107.

21 Fri: Benjamin Disraeli, b. 1804; Giovanni Boccaccio, d. 1375; Independence Day, Nepal.

22 Sat: Noel Edmonds, b. 1948; Ralph Fiennes, b. 1962; George Eliot, d. 1880.

23 Sun: Frederick Augustus I of Saxony, b. 1750; Jodie Marsh, b. 1978; Charles Atlas, d. 1973.

24 Mon: Colin Cowdrey, b. 1932; Carol Vorderman, b, 1960; Vasco da Gama, d. 1524.

25 Tues: Annie Lennox, b. 1954; Helena Christensen, b. 1968; W. C. Fields, d. 1946.

26 Wed: Phil Spector, b. 1940; Jack Benny, d. 1974; Good Will Day, South Africa.

27 Thurs: Louis Pasteur, b. 1822; Duncan Ferguson, b. 1971; Hoagy Carmichael, d. 1981.

28 Fri: Roy Hattersley, b. 1932; Sienna Miller, b. 1981; Antipope Clement VIII, d. 1446.

29 Sat: W. E. Gladstone, b. 1809; Aled Jones, b. 1970; Thomas a Becket, d. 1170.

30 Sun: Bo Diddley, b. 1928; Robert Boyle, d. 1691; Rizal Day, Philippines.

31 Mon: Anthony Hopkins, b. 1937; Donna Summer, b. 1948; Margrave Ottokar III of Styria, d. 1164.

Weather forecast for December: Some areas of Britain may see rain of varying amounts while others may remain dry from time to time. There will be some sunshine in certain places, particularly where the clouds break, as well as a risk of thunder and maybe fog. Where trees start blowing about, it will be windy. Snow, sleet and hail are also possible but may not happen at all. Temperatures will be around, above or below normal. It will generally be dark at night, but lighter by day. A plague of locusts will sweep across Basildon on the 8th.

IMPORTANT ANNIVERSARIES FOR 2007

1st anniversary of 2006.

20th anniversary of a Middlesex woman passing her driving test at the 49th attempt.

25th anniversary of Renée and Renato topping the UK charts with 'Save Your Love'.

26th anniversary of the beginning and end of Welsh TV soap Taff Acre.

29th anniversary of Canada's Pat Donahue eating ninety-one pickled onions in just over a minute.

30th anniversary of the Conservatives winning the Saffron Walden by-election.

40th anniversary of the grand founding of Milton Keynes.

45th anniversary of Ken Barlow's marriage to Valerie Tatlock in Coronation Street.

50th anniversary of the manufacture of the Frisbee.

60th anniversary of John Plant winning the Swiss Amateur Golf Championship.

61st anniversary of the deposition of King Zog of Albania.

62nd anniversary of the invention of Tupperware by Earl Silas Tupper.

70th anniversary of the launch of Spam.

72nd anniversary of Mickey Mouse being banned in Romania.

80th anniversary of the invention of the pop-up toaster by Charles Strite.

87th anniversary of the opening of the Panama Canal.

90th anniversary of the invention of TCP by Romanian biochemist Count Callimachi.

94th anniversary of the discovery of the crested shelduck in Korea.

96th anniversary of the instance of a 2-foot-long alligator falling from the sky at Evansville, Indiana and landing on the front doorstep of the home of Mrs Hiram Winchell.

100th anniversary of the first London taxis with meters.

103rd anniversary of the solitary appearance of roque (an American variation of croquet) in the Olympics.

107th anniversary of the invention of the paper clip by Norwegian Johann Vaaler.

131st anniversary of the overthrow of Ottoman Sultan Murad V.

133rd anniversary of the invention of barbed wire by American Lucien B. Smith.

185th anniversary of the first false teeth patent.

200th anniversary of the discovery of the asteroid Vesta by H.W. Olbers.

300th anniversary of the publication of *Arithmetica Universalis*, the collected works of Isaac Newton on algebra.

341st anniversary of the Great Fire of London.

411th anniversary of the death of Sir Francis Drake.

480th anniversary of the possible first sighting of the Loch Ness Monster.

486th anniversary of the Diet of Worms.

500th anniversary of the Portuguese occupation of the island of Lamu.

792nd anniversary of the Magna Carta.

941st anniversary of the Battle of Hastings.

987th anniversary of Oliver of Malmesbury's attempt to become the first man in the world to fly. Although he failed to break any records, he did break a leg.

1,000th anniversary of the death of Spanish mathematician Al Madshritti.

WORLDWIDE TROPICAL CYCLONE NAMES FOR 2007

Andrea	Barry
Chantal	Dean
Erin	Felix
Gabrielle	Humberto
Ingrid	Jerry
Karen	Lorenzo
Melissa	Noel
Olga	Pablo
Rebekah	Sebastien
Tanya	Van
Wendy	

NOTABLE BIRTHDAYS IN 2007

Romeo Beckham, 5
Ronan Keating, 30
Davina McCall, 40
Shane McGowan, 50
Sooty, 59
Arnold Schwarzenegger, 60
Robert Redford, 70
Andy Williams, 80
Jane Russell, 86
George Bernard Shaw, 151
King Alfonso XI of Leon and Castile, 695

NEW UK COLLEGE COURSES FOR 2007

Following the news that Bridgend College in South Wales has started a degree course for Elvis impersonators, an exciting range of new subjects has opened up for UK students in 2007. They include:

Waiting at a bus stop
Advanced breathing
Peeing up a wall
Yawning
Letting your hair grow
Practical fidgeting
Ant and Dec
Balancing a beer mat on the end of your nose
Piling up dishes in a sink
Hollyoaks
Sitting around thinking of something to do

WORLD DAYS FOR 2007
(to be confirmed)

5 January: World Eat Your Vegetables Day

31 January: World Grumbling Day

8 February: World Yo-Yo Day

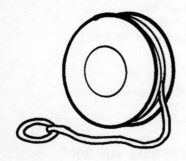

17 February: World Gnat Day

23 March: World Chutney Day

29 March: World Abuse Your Bank Manager Day

2 April: World Varicose Veins Day

12 April: World Supermarket Trolley Day

22 April: World Salad Dressing Day

5 May: World Speak Only Japanese Day

16 May: World Don't Be So Cheeky To Your Sister Day

25 May: World Milk Float Day

10 June: World Cello Day

20 June: World Darren Day Day

7 July: World Rice Pudding Day

13 July: World Don't Forget To Wash Behind Your Ears Day

29 July: World Duck-billed Platypus Day

2 August: World Garden Decking Day

24 August: World Boomerang Day

28 August: World Help An Old Lady Into The Road Day

7 September: World Thong Day

18 September: World Ear Hair Day

11 October: World No Farting Day

15 October: World Apathy Day*

10 November: World Lovely Debbie McGee Day

24 November: World Malteser Day

1 December: World Slap Anyone With A Clipboard Day

15 December: World Grazed Finger Day

27 December: World Shave Your Gerbil Day

* may be cancelled

STARS FOR THE STARS

George W. Bush

Happy-go-lucky George has been President of the United States since 2000 and is generally considered to be the most powerful – although not necessarily the most intelligent – man in the world.

George was born on 6 July 1946 and, as a typical Cancer, is often headstrong, short and stupid. Cancer is an emotional water sign, and George's tenure of office has indeed been enough to reduce many Americans to tears. The link between his Moon and Saturn indicates that he comes from a close-knit family - as George himself remarked recently: 'We are the closest knits in the whole of Texas.'

In George's sign, Mercury (the planet for communication and thinking) is linked with Uranus, as a result of which he frequently talks out of his arse. With Pluto away on holiday at the time that he was born, George can struggle to put words together coherently. Alternatively, this trait may have been caused by a bump on the head at an early age. The positioning of Neptune in this planetary order suggests that George also suffers from feelings of inadequacy, which would appear to be wholly justified. It has been claimed that George surrounds himself with capable individuals in order to hide his own shortcomings, but one look at Dick Cheney and Donald Rumsfeld conclusively disproves this theory.

So what does 2007 hold for George? With Mercury dissing Mars in a row over Leo, the start of the year brings more bad news for George, to the extent that his popularity rating could disappear off the radar altogether. March could be a period of consolidation, and a relatively quiet period in the last two weeks of April gives George the opportunity to learn some new words. However, this respite may be short-lived because with bully-boy Saturn contacting all of George's planets in Gemini during June, further turbulent times lie ahead. Those closest to him will advise him to curb his impetuosity by counting to ten before making important decisions. Unfortunately, George can count only up to eight at the moment, and he can't manage even that if he is wearing mittens. With new scandals threatening to engulf his administration, September could see George fleeing the country by night in a rowing boat.

Jade Goody

Since appearing on *Big Brother* in 2002, Jade has enjoyed her fifteen minutes of fame several times over, thus confounding her critics, who snipe that undergoing root canal surgery without an anaesthetic is preferable to watching the former dental nurse in action.

Jade was born on 5 June 1981 at a time when both the Sun and Mercury were occupying her zodiac sign of Gemini. This alignment has contributed to her colourful, sometimes volatile, lifestyle, and to her general philosophy, since Mercury is widely regarded as being the planet of the chav. Along with many Geminis, Jade often lives with her head in the clouds, a characteristic demonstrated at the 2006 London Marathon when, after training on a diet of curry and booze, she unsurprisingly failed to complete the course, groaning, 'I'm dying, I'm dying' as she was helped away. Half of the population thought she must be on another planet; the other half wished she actually was. Such judgements are of course grossly unfair, for Jade is a source of inspiration to us all. If somebody with no discernible talent and the sort of face usually seen attached to a fishing hook can make a fortune, there is hope for everyone. And with Pluto seeing Capricorn so regularly that they are almost engaged, Jade knows no shame. Despite being voted number four in Channel 4's 100 Worst Britons poll, she possesses indefatigable spirit. Quite simply, Jade doesn't know the meaning of the word 'defeat', although it has to be said this is just one of hundreds of words she doesn't know the meaning of. Therefore, no matter what life – or anyone – throws at her, she always bounces back.

For the first few months of 2007 Jade will continue to feature regularly as a magazine centrefold, if only because hers is one of the few faces that can actually be improved by having a staple through the middle. But around 11 April, Jupiter may threaten to resign from the solar system and the resulting uncertainty could affect Jade's career. Because hers is an Air sign – indeed many consider her to be the Air head – her mental fortitude will be needed to see her through this tricky period. Jade could find fresh opportunities to revive her fortunes in October, possibly presenting a new daytime game show involving sheep.

Jerry Springer

The popular London-born talk-show host has made a career out of
encouraging people to air their private problems before an
audience of millions in what is the modern equivalent of the
Roman Colosseum.

Born on 13 February 1944, Jerry is a typical Aquarian, always
fishing in muddy waters, both as a politician and as a journalist.
The influence of Mars (the ego planet) in his chart is clear for all to
see, but weekend visits from Neptune add the sympathetic air that
encourages guests to see him as a confidant and gives them the
courage to make complete jerks of themselves on national
television. The fact that they are invariably just one step above
plant life on the intellectual ladder also helps.

The positioning of the planets indicates that 2007 will be
another lively year for Jerry. In the third week of February he will
meet a Wyoming man who has been having sex with his brother,
his sister-in-law, his mother and her horse. With Saturn sticking its
nose in everybody's business, the first week of May will see Jerry
refereeing a marital dispute between a man who believes he is the
reincarnation of his grandmother's Alsatian and a woman who is
convinced that she was a lamppost in a former life. Around 11
August it is possible that Jerry will encounter a man who loves to
wrap his entire body in Clingfilm and consequently hasn't been to
the toilet for three years. But there is a cloud on Jerry's horizon: in
the first week in November he will be confronted with a happily
married couple who have no hang-ups, quarrels or sexual
deviations, and he simply won't know what to say.

Tony Blair

Ever-cheerful Tony became British Prime Minister in 1997, but in
recent years he would be the first to admit that he has had
precious little to smile about.

Tony was born on 6 May 1953 at a time when Neptune was
behaving like a spoilt child, and it is this planetary neglect that has
given him such unrelenting optimism. After that inauspicious start
in life, things, as Tony is wont to say, could only get better. As a
Taurus, Tony has always been practical: look how he has learned
to play the guitar and run the country at the same time.

His being an Earth sign, Tony also enjoys walking in the garden of 10 Downing Street and breaking bad news to cabinet ministers. If he can combine sacking a Home Secretary with a spot of weeding, all the better. But when dismissing Charles Clarke, he was unable to hold back the tears after noticing the first sign of blackspot on the roses. The presence of Mercury and Mars in Pisces guarantees that water plays a key role in Tony's life. For much of 2006, however, the Piscean water combined with the Taurus earth to form a messy brown sludge from which Tony struggled to extricate himself.

The year 2007 looks to be one of major changes for Tony and he will need every ounce of his legendary charm to ride the storm. The omens are particularly poor around the third week of February. Mars is in a strop, Saturn is given a solar system ASBO for persistent unruly behaviour and the Sun brings bad news when Rupert Murdoch withdraws his support. Also, Cherie forgets Valentine's Day. April may be a time for renewed optimism, but Tony should be wary of placing too much trust on anyone in a kilt. Neptune is fidgety throughout August and this restlessness may lead to Tony seeking (or being asked to seek) a new job. Influences in Gemini and Libra may govern his decision, while Tony's astrological chart also suggests problems with Leo in the future, but that's teenagers for you.

PUNTER'S GUIDE TO HORSE RACING
(based on detailed astrological predictions)

Jockeys to follow in 2007:
Frankie Dettori, Kieran Fallon, Jamie Spencer,
Richard Quinn, Mick Fitzgerald, Tony McCoy

Jockeys not to follow in 2007:
Lester Piggott, Willie Carson, Gordon Richards,
Peter Scudamore, Dick Francis

EXCITING NEW TOYS FOR 2007

Litigation: A great board game in which you can sue your parents for any perceived inadequacies or contest a relative's will. Fun for all the family.

Wayne Rooney Doll: Wind him up and watch him explode. Comes with removable brain.

Cancelled Operation: A compelling new version of the old favourite, in which players throw a dice to discover when a hospital bed will eventually become available. A game of chance.

Trivial Police Pursuit: Players compete to see who can initiate the most pointless prosecution. The winner gets to be 'Chief Constable'.

Inaction Man: Kids will have hours of fun trying to make this couch potato move. Accessories include TV remote control, beer can and electric cattle prod.

Happy Dysfunctional Families: A new variation on the popular card game. The loser is the one left with the 'Social Worker'.

A clothes peg (top) converted into a paper clip (bottom).

The only operations required are to make two fresh notches for the spring arms, and to turn the spring around.

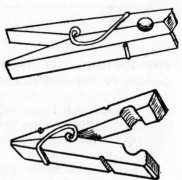

SHOPPER'S CHART FOR 2007

January
A good time to pick up bargains in the sales, but beware of buying any old tat as funds may be low after Christmas. The omens are positive for leather, negative for chiffon. Best shopping days: 6th, 10th, 13th, 26th. Bad shopping day: 21st.

February
An excellent month for buying curtains and lampshades. Favoured colours: chocolate brown and rust; avoid green unless you like it. Best shopping days: 16th, 22nd, 25th. Bad shopping day: 9th.

March
There has never been a better time for buying verruca gel. But be quick: stocks may run out after the 12th. Best shopping days: 5th, 7th, 10th. Bad shopping days: 19th, 20th.

April
Time to start planning your summer wardrobe, but think twice before buying any clothes that aren't your size. Best shopping days: 14th, 17th, 29th. Bad shopping day: 1st.

May
There is likely to be a sofa sale within a mile of wherever you live, but remember it must end soon. Best shopping days: 4th, 30th. Bad shopping day: 11th.

June
The signs are favourable for most types of shopping, but especially for household goods and anything on your husband's credit card. Store muzak will almost certainly be irritating. Best shopping days: 3rd, 9th, 25th. Bad shopping days: None.

July
A good month for buying shoes, but not the assortment of buffers and cleaners they always try to sell you at the same time. Lucky price tag: £69.99. Best shopping days: 7th, 15th, 24th, 25th. Bad shopping days: 6th, 31st.

August

Traditionally this is the best month of the year for buying kettles, so don't pass up the opportunity. Sales staff may be rude because they're not on holiday. Best shopping days: 20th, 21st, 27th. Bad shopping days: 7th, 14th.

September

The positioning of the planets indicates fuzzy barcodes, which means that you should restrict shopping to bare essentials, certainly for the first two weeks of the month. Rather than risk incurring the wrath of the shopping gods, try buying over the Internet. It may be safe to venture out towards the end of the month when you could treat yourself to a nice cream cake. Best shopping day: 28th. Bad shopping days: 2nd, 5th, 6th, 9th, 10th, 13th, 14th.

October

Since the 3rd is St Tracey's Day (the patron saint of supermarket checkout assistants), the portents are wholesome for food shopping. Best shopping days: 5th, 10th, 23rd. Bad shopping day: 19th.

November

With the nights drawing in and another expensive Christmas approaching, the time couldn't be better for a spot of shoplifting. Watch out for store detectives and snarling dogs. Best shopping days: 4th, 9th, 25th. Bad shopping days: 12th, 16th.

December

Important decisions have to be made regarding Christmas presents. Should you buy Uncle Jim socks for the eighth year running? And does Cousin Jane really deserve that 'Roundabouts of Britain' tea towel you were given last year? Best shopping days: 6th, 9th, 14th. Bad shopping day: 25th (everything's closed).

CHINESE ZODIAC

The year 2007 marks the start of the Chinese Year of the Pig, one of the twelve signs of the Chinese zodiac. Check out the personality traits associated with each sign.

Rat: Those born in the Year of the Rat are cunning, resourceful and natural survivors. They also have a fondness for cheese. Rats' ideal partners are cockerels, but they should steer clear of tigers and snakes who may eat them alive. Likely occupation: journalist. Famous rats: Prince Charles, Diego Maradona.

Ox: People born in the Year of the Ox are hard-working and reliable, although somewhat lacking in finesse. Ideal companions are horses and a cart. Likely occupation: Sumo wrestler. Famous oxen: Monica Lewinsky, Margaret Thatcher.

Tiger: Tigers are habitually loners who shun human contact. This can make them difficult to tame for prospective partners. Their ideal companions are snakes. Likely occupation: soldier (they quickly earn their stripes). Famous tigers: Karl Marx, Groucho Marx.

Rabbit: Those born in the Year of the Rabbit are passionate to the point of being sex machines. But they can get twitchy at the thought of commitment. Their perfect partners are anything with a pulse. Likely occupation: entertainer. Famous rabbits: David Beckham, Brad Pitt.

Dragon: Dragons are fiery individuals who tend to blow hot and cold. They should avoid anyone called George. Likely occupation: seaside landlady. Famous dragons: Roseanne Barr, Sandra Bullock.

Snake: People born in the Year of the Snake must be handled with caution, not least because they can spread poison and tend to speak with a forked tongue. Likely occupation: politician. Famous snakes: Alex Ferguson, Tony Blair.

Horse: Horses are traditionally fast movers, as a result of which they don't like being saddled with trivial problems. And they can be blinkered to their own faults. Ideal partner: Frankie Dettori. Likely occupation: horse impersonator. Famous horses: Sean Connery, Jordan.

Sheep: Those born in the Year of the Sheep are invariably followers rather than trailblazers. They also tend to worry and this can lead to sleepless nights, the best solution for which is to count their blessings. In terms of relationships, they get on well with pigs and cockerels, but can be intimidated by dogs, who tend to push them into a corner. Likely occupation: anything you suggest. Famous sheep: Bruce Willis, Bill Gates.

Monkey: Monkeys are born clowns, but whilst high in entertainment value, they make unreliable partners because they are renowned swingers. They should avoid tigers at all costs. Likely occupation: banana-grower. Famous monkeys: Tom Hanks, Ronaldinho.

Cockerel: Those born in the Year of the Cockerel are proud and self-important, fond of making a lot of noise about very little. They are famously early to rise and may have a funny walk. Ideal partner: a mirror. Likely occupation: hairdresser. Famous cocks: Errol Flynn, James Brown.

Dog: Anyone born in the Year of the Dog tends to be loyal and loving but sometimes over-excitable. They like to leave their mark on society – and often on the pavement. Sleeping dogs may lie, so don't pay attention to anything they say in their dreams. Ideal partners are rabbits, although for the dog the thrill is often in the chase. Likely occupation: model. Famous dogs: Madonna, Sophia Loren.

Pig: People born in the Year of the Pig are by nature food lovers, scrupulously clean and with little curly tails. Their ideal partner is apple sauce. Likely occupation: police officer. Famous pigs: Hillary Rodham Clinton, Al Capone.

FOOTBALL POOLS: YOUR LUCKY TEAMS FOR 2007

This forecast, based on a combination of planetary indications, team colours and sticking a pin in a list of names, reveals the teams most likely to draw on the dates given, regardless of whether or not they are actually playing that day. Furthermore, Old Shite accepts no legal responsibility for any failure to win, so don't start bombarding us with angry letters again. Basically, readers should use their own judgement, because most of these will be wrong. Your home may be at risk if you do not keep up with payments.

6 January
Macclesfield, Barnsley, Luton

13 January
Hull, Watford, Macclesfield

20 January
Queens Park Rangers, Macclesfield, Arsenal

27 January
Manchester City, Oldham, Macclesfield

3 February
Macclesfield, Chelsea, Rochdale

10 February
Millwall, Notts County, Macclesfield

17 February
Bristol Rovers, Brighton, Macclesfield

24 February
Aberdeen, Macclesfield, Port Vale

3 March
Stoke City, Sunderland, Macclesfield

10 March
Accrington Stanley, Macclesfield, Spurs

17 March
Macclesfield, Bradford, Bournemouth

24 March
Hearts, Macclesfield, Lincoln

31 March
Mansfield, West Ham, Macclesfield

7 April
Swansea, Wrexham, Macclesfield

14 April
Crystal Palace, Ipswich, Macclesfield

21 April
Plymouth, Macclesfield, Bolton

28 April
Liverpool, Macclesfield, Reading

5 May
Macclesfield, Coventry, Doncaster

4 August
Stenhousemuir, Huddersfield, Macclesfield

11 August
Shrewsbury, Macclesfield, Forfar

18 August
Nottingham Forest, Everton, Macclesfield

25 August
Blackburn, Macclesfield, Peterborough

1 September
Macclesfield, Leyton Orient, St Mirren

8 September
Celtic, Wolves, Macclesfield

15 September
Rotherham, Macclesfield, Manchester United

22 September
Swindon, Gretna, Macclesfield

29 September
Sheffield United, Preston, Macclesfield

6 October
Tranmere, Macclesfield, Brechin

13 October
Macclesfield, Cardiff, Kilmarnock

20 October
Aston Villa, Macclesfield, Bristol Rovers

27 October
Brentford, Hartlepool, Macclesfield

3 November
Gillingham, St Johnstone, Macclesfield

10 November
Southend, MK Dons, Macclesfield

17 November
Macclesfield, Chester, Arbroath

24 November
Northampton, Montrose, Macclesfield

1 December
Leeds, Dundee, Macclesfield

8 December
East Stirling, Macclesfield, Fulham

15 December
Bury, Carlisle, Macclesfield

22 December
Partick Thistle, Macclesfield, Hamilton

29 December
Ayr United, Southampton, Macclesfield

Summary
Team to follow: Middlesbrough

BEST SOWING AND PLANTING TIMES FOR THE GARDEN IN 2007

Success in raising healthy flowers and vegetables relies on soil care, meticulous planning, skill and patience, favourable weather conditions and, above all, the mood of next door's cat. Using the phases of the moon and the positioning of the planets as our guide, we predict how next door's cat will behave in 2007 and therefore which are the best times to sow and plant.

January
The cold weather means that next door's cat will spend most of the month curled up in a warm place. So plant cabbages on the afternoon of the 24th unless you've got something interesting to do.

February
Next door's cat will still be feeling drowsy and mainly staying indoors. Sow peas and beans between 2.36 p.m. and 3.13 p.m. on the 9th.

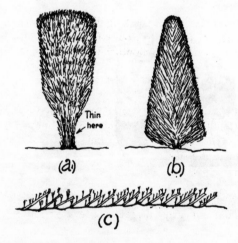

(a) Hedge trimmed wrongly; result, thin at bottom.
(b) Hedge trimmed on the taper; thick all the way up.
(c) Sets placed obliquely to overlap; shoots grow vertically.

March
Spring is in the air towards the end of the month and next door's cat will be venturing into your garden. But he is usually fed around 5 p.m., so sneak out and sow spinach seeds when he is not looking.

April
Next door's cat will now be spending most days in your garden, spraying against blackspot, mildew and your shed. But it's still a bit cold for him to go out at night, so plant celery between 2.06 a.m. and 3.25 a.m. on the 19th.

May
This month next door's cat will be watching your every move, relishing the opportunity to roll in freshly raked soil the moment you've sown seeds. Fortunately, there's a film on Channel 4 that he wants to watch on the 16th, so make the most of his absence by sowing cucumber and lettuce.

June
Next door's cat will now be making the most of the long summer nights by virtually taking up twenty-four-hour residence in your garden. All you can do this month is water any surviving plants before he does.

July
With next door's cat being carted off to the cattery for the last two weeks in July, cancel your own holiday and sow turnips and radishes for an autumn crop. By the time he returns, they will have gained a solid start.

August
Next door's cat will be rampant following his enforced incarceration. Plant early cabbages and leeks at your peril.

September
This is the classic mouse-hunting month for next door's cat, but he will be in trouble on the 19th for taking one of his catches into his owner's bedroom. He may be feeling wounded and chastened, so take advantage of his uncharacteristically subdued mood and sow broccoli seeds relentlessly from the 20th onwards.

October
Next door's cat will be winding down for the winter, allowing you a window to plant radishes on the morning of the 27th.

November
Next door's cat won't be let out on Bonfire Night, so brave the rockets and Roman candles to plant late cabbages by torchlight.

December
Next door's cat will be having a lie-in on the 10th, so that gives you a chance to plant yet more bloody cabbages and prepare the soil in readiness for forthcoming conflicts. To help protect your seeds and plants in 2008, buy your wife a pitbull for Christmas.

REVIEW OF THE YEAR TO COME

January

The Pyramids are found to be made of plastic.

Britain's fishing industry is in crisis
after someone accidentally pulls the
plug out of the North Sea.

Lego offers to complete the building of Wembley Stadium.

Jeremy Kyle confesses to dressing up as a nun at weekends.

Tony Christie finally gets SatNav to help him find the way to
Amarillo.

February

In a surprise by-election result, Bez of the Happy Mondays is
elected Conservative MP for East Grinstead.

The *Deal Or No Deal* audience joins hands in a determined
exhibition of positive thinking. It works: Noel Edmonds disappears.

Victoria Beckham buys Yorkshire.

March

Ming Campbell wakes up to find that he has become leader of the
Liberal Democrats.

Grateful seal pups prevent the culling of Heather Mills McCartney.

Osama bin Laden is found working at the Home Office.

April

Edd the Duck and Gordon the Gopher are arrested for brawling in a Soho bar.

As the McCartney divorce becomes increasingly acrimonious, Heather demands that Paul keep the rights to everything he has recorded since the Beatles, particularly 'Wonderful Christmastime', 'Ebony and Ivory' and 'We All Stand Together'.

Lord Lucan and Glenn Miller are discovered playing cards with Shergar and the crew of the *Mary Celeste* at an Isle of Wight boarding house.

May

Fathers 4 Justice invade the stage at the Eurovision Song Contest, screaming and shouting obscenities. They finish second.

Water, water, everywhere and not a drop to drink, as Thames Water unveils its new policy.

Among the housemates for the new series of *Big Brother* are a one-legged transsexual with Alzheimer's, a pantomime horse and a corpse.

An army of triffids storm the Chelsea Flower Show and abduct Alan Titchmarsh. He is later released in exchange for a £10 garden-centre token and a bottle of Baby Bio.

June

Tim Henman loses to Ronnie Corbett in the first round at Wimbledon.

As high seas batter the Cornish coast, a seventy-five-year-old Bude man unintentionally becomes the first person to cross the Atlantic in a deckchair.

July

The Footsie will have a good day on the 16th. It's going to Alton Towers with the Dow Jones.

Liam Gallagher records a duet with Moira Anderson.

McDonald's opens a branch on the summit of Mount Everest.

August

Sven-Göran Eriksson returns to English football as manager of Bridlington Town.

A large section of the Polar icecap is seen floating up the Nile.

Geri Halliwell turns down an opportunity to appear in *Hello!* magazine.

September

The Bank of England orders a 1 per cent rise in interest rates and that Howard from the Halifax be humanely put down.

Saddam Hussein is released on special licence to appear on *Celebrity Stars in their Eyes* as Bobby Crush. Afterwards, Saddam manages to escape from his guards – an assistant floor manager and a make-up girl – and assume Bobby Crush's identity.

October

Confusion reigns as Bobby Crush stands trial in Baghdad for his crimes against humanity – namely the albums *All Time Piano Hits*, *Piano Party* and *Honky Tonk Favourites*.

The football world is rocked by the revelation that Peter Crouch is really two men welded together.

November

Vanessa Feltz sinks.

Penge declares independence from the rest of London.

Saddam Hussein is finally re-arrested following a successful matinee performance at the Palace Theatre, Morecambe.

December

A pair of John Prescott's old underpants win the Turner Prize.

Paul McCartney marries Girls Aloud.

It emerges that George W. Bush has been clinically dead for ten years.

IMPORTANT DATES FOR YOUR 2007 CALENDAR

January

International Snow Sculpting Championships, Colorado.

National Cowboy Poetry Gathering, Nevada.

Oatman Bed Race, Arizona.

February

World Snow Shovel Race, New Mexico.

Camel Beauty Pageant, United Arab Emirates.

National Penny-farthing Championships, Evandale, Tasmania.

March

Odor-eaters International Rotten Sneaker Championships, Vermont.

Cardboard Box Derby, Colorado.

April

Underwater Music Festival, Florida.

Cardboard Boat Regatta, Arizona.

Interstate Mullet Toss, Florida.

World Moon Rock Throwing Championships, Richmond, Queensland.

Australian Tractor Pull Championships, Quambatook, Victoria.

Pig Olympics, Russia.

May

World Bog Snorkelling Championships, Llanwrtyd Wells, Powys.

World Cheese Rolling Championships, Birdlip, Gloucestershire.

International Lobster Race, Aiken, South Carolina.

Calveras County Jumping Frog Championships, California.

O. Henry World Pun Championships, Austin, Texas.

June

World Toe Wrestling Championships, Wetton, Staffordshire.

World Egg Throwing Championships, Swaton, Lincolnshire.

World Shin Kicking Championships, Chipping Campden, Gloucestershire.

National Hollerin' Contest, Spivey's Corner, North Carolina.

Beer Can Regatta, Darwin, Australia.

Wife Carrying World Championships, Helsinki.

July

World Worm Charming Championships, Willaston, Cheshire.

World Snail Racing Championships, Congham, Norfolk.

Vancouver Bathtub Race.

International Hot Dog Eating Contest, New York.

Hubcap Hurling Championships, Georgia.

World Pillow Fighting Championships, California.

International Cherry Pit Spitting Contest, Eau Claire, Michigan.

Annual Bear Creek Saloon Pig Race, Montana.

World's Greatest Lizard Race, Lovington, New Mexico.

International Brick Throwing Championships, Stroud, New South Wales.

Moose Dropping Festival, Talkeetna, Alaska.

Watermelon Day, Minnesota.

August

World Flounder Tramping Championships, Urr Estuary, Scotland.

World Plank Walking Championships, Isle of Sheppey.

World Sauna Sitting Championships, Heinola, Finland.

September

World Black Pudding Knocking Championships, Ramsbottom, Lancashire.

World Beard and Moustache Championships, Brighton, Sussex.

World Gurning Championships, Egremont, Cumbria.

Bald is Beautiful Convention, North Carolina.

Running of the Sheep, Reedpoint, Montana.

Great Topeka Rubber Duck Race, Lake Shawnee, Kansas.

Great Klondike Outhouse Race, Dawson City, Canada.

National Sheep Counting Championships, Hay, New South Wales.

World Air Guitar Championships, Oulu, Finland.

World Testicle Cooking Championships, Serbia.

October

National Phone Texting Championships, London.

Pumpkin Paddling Regatta, Windsor, Nova Scotia.

Emma Crawford Coffin Races, Manitou Springs, Colorado.

National Yo-yo Championships, California.

Festival of Scarecrows, Maine.

Great Klondike Outhouse Race, Dawson City, Canada.

Henley-on-Todd Regatta, Alice Springs.

European Lawn Mower Championships, Limoges, France.

November

World Duck Calling Championships, Stuttgart, Arkansas.

Palm Desert Golf Cart Parade, California.

World Pole Sitting Championships, Soltau, Germany.

December

Night of the Radishes, Oaxaca, Mexico.

World Elephant-polo Championships, Nepal.